The Seve
Prac

by

The Seven Pillars of a Painless Practice
Practice Development for Practitioners
by James Butler and Celia Champion

Published by:
Painless Limited
31 Station Road
Cholsey
OX10 9PT
United Kingdom

01491 659073
www.painlesspractice.com

First published in 2012
Copyright © Painless Limited 2012

About the Authors

James Butler and Celia Champion are directors of Painless Practice, which offers a range of support for practitioners – including a free monthly newsletter by email, workshops, training courses, practice health checks and direct support and coaching for practice owners, practice managers and associates. The Painless name derives from a deeply held belief that making a living should be as free from pain as possible – a sentiment many practitioners will identify with. Sometimes all that is required is a review of the experience a patient has, sometimes a strategic review of practice management, often it is an objective and supportive sounding board to talk through plans and options, providing an external voice of reason.

Prior to working in this field, James built a successful business in the environmental sector and since 2002 he has worked on helping business owners, especially practitioners, to build better practices. He has worked with hundreds of clients, over thousands of hours in dozens of sectors. He has written two other books on practice development and speaks widely on the topic. He has worked on programmes for business owners at both Cranfield School of Management and Cass Business School.

Celia's professional career started in South Africa, where she grew up. She built a successful business in the security industry, before selling the firm and becoming a Managing Director within the new parent company. For many years, her talent and passion was developing people in her team to improve themselves and the business, so when she relocated with her family to the UK it was natural that she would want to work as a coach, trainer and facilitator. She joined Painless Practice and since then has accelerated the growth of the business, worked one-to-one with many clients, lectured widely and is a respected authority on practice development for practitioners.

www	www.painlesspractice.com
	www.twitter.com/celiachampion
	http://www.linkedin.com/groups?gid=3324659
	www.facebook.com/pages/Painless-Practice/150394674987062

Painless Practice is a trading name of Painless Limited. Registered in England: 5362019. VAT No: 993 6996 33

Contents

Acknowledgements

We have a lot of people to thank, firstly for the opportunity to work with practitioners, and secondly for help in the preparation of this book.

Painless Practice may not exist without the friendship between James and Sara Kennard, who first raised the possibility of working with osteopaths to help them improve their practices. From that germ of an idea, a very fruitful relationship with the British Osteopathic Association has developed, particularly with Michael Watson and Catherine Goodyear. From that connection came James' first book, the BOA's Business Development Handbook.

Our next debt is to Sarah Whittaker, a talented homeopath and an amazing woman, and the collaborator on Running a Successful Homeopathic Practice, published by the Society of Homeopaths. We must also thank Rob Finch of the College of Chiropractors for his insight and suggested improvements to the Seven Pillars – putting patients in their rightful place at the centre.

Thanks are due to Gerard Burke, the rest of the Your Business Your Future team, and to the participants on the Better Business Programme. We learn something from every encounter with them, and it is generous and gracious of Gerard to allow us to apply the idea of Seven Pillars in a different way to a different sector.

We both consider ourselves lucky to work in this field. We take huge delight in seeing those we work with develop themselves and their businesses, and we find the therapy sector an enjoyable sector to specialise in. Whether through idle chats at conferences, interactions on our workshops, one-to-ones with clients or exercises during in-practice training events with clinics, we are always learning about the professions and what makes practices successful. This book represents that collective knowledge.

We are also grateful for Vicky, Hugh, Ann and Tracey, who contribute so much to the success of Painless Practice, and who help us extend our reach to hundreds and hundreds of practitioners each year.

A project like this also involves unsung heroes, who tediously and meticulously ensure we minimise the typos, errors and inconsistencies. Thanks to Bev Butler, Carol Plumridge, Michael Palfrey, Heather Barron, Naomi Watkins and Chris Johnson who have provided that input – especially from a practitioner's viewpoint. As always, any errors that remain are our responsibility alone.

Finally, we thank you, the reader, for taking the trouble to buy the book and to read it. This shows you want to develop a stronger foundation for your clinic – we hope the Seven Pillars provide you with that foundation.

Introduction

Why this book?

If you are holding this book in your hands, either having bought it, or because you are considering buying it, it is likely that you want your practice to be better in some way than it is now. Perhaps you haven't started it yet and are planning the launch, or perhaps you have been running it for years, and want some fresh impetus. Either way, this book is written with you in mind.

At Painless Practice our purpose is to see business owners enjoying their work and achieving their vision, and to that end we have been working with health practitioners to build better practices since 2004. Very early on, it was clear that most practitioners had well-developed technical ability in their field, but often lacked any training, experience or confidence in the business side of their clinic. This held back their ability to grow the number of patients they served, affecting their livelihood and well-being, and reducing the beneficial impact on the health and vitality of the communities they sought to serve.

We have worked with (in no particular order) osteopaths, chiropractors, physiotherapists, occupational therapists, speech and language therapists, homeopaths, nutritional practitioners, acupuncturists, Bowen practitioners, reflexologists, holistic practitioners, GPs and many others, and the same issues have arisen. As it happens, we have worked with many other industries including graphic designers, surveyors, distributors, software houses, printers, importers, builders and butchers (but no bakers or candlestick makers, from memory), and the story is no different.

This book is our attempt to start to redress that balance, specifically for health practitioners. We have written two separate similar books, one aimed only at osteopaths, the other purely at homeopaths, but this is a general text for anyone in any health-based private practice. Perhaps a further book will serve the butchers and bakers, but we have chosen to keep this one focussed.

Carefully chosen words

While we talk of the target for this book, it may help to clarify some terminology. We hear our client base variously described as complementary or alternative. Individuals may be described as practitioners, therapists, or by their profession – as we did earlier. For some, the exact word is important, and there can be an emotional reaction if the wrong one is used. We cannot, however, litter the book with clunky catch-alls like practitioner/therapist/healer, and so we have decided to use practitioner throughout. Similarly, we have consistently referred to patients, though we are aware that some will prefer clients, and we have used treatment when others might use consultation. We have interchanged practice and clinic, depending on what we felt worked at that point. Please bear with us – we hope that overall it will help the flow of the text.

On a related note, we will often refer to successful clinics in this book. We have no definition of what success is. For each and every practitioner we have worked with, success has been defined differently – depending on their hopes, dreams and aspirations. We have worked with successful practitioners who have a clinic providing 10 treatments a week – whilst they raise their children or wind down to retirement. We have also met and worked with practitioners for whom a clinic of 20 practitioners, providing 1000 treatments a week, is a definition of success. Both are right – because success is defined on their terms. With this book, you will work on defining what it means for you.

The structure of the book

Our purpose with this book is to provide an easy-to-use reference guide and workbook for any practitioner wanting to improve their practice. We have structured the book around our Seven Pillars – useful mental hooks upon which to hang the many tips and exercises we want to share with you. Each section will have exercises for you to consider – giving you immediate benefits you can start to implement in your clinic. Alternatively, you can bring them all together in the Plan Pillar: your plan for your better practice.

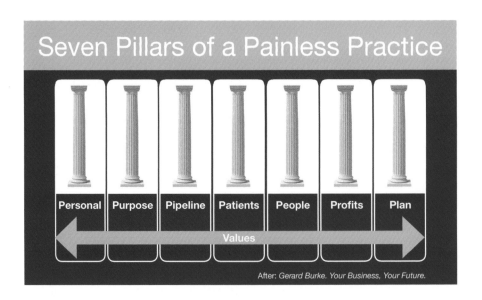

After: *Gerard Burke. Your Business, Your Future.*

As the Seven Pillars form the skeleton for the book, and the chapter headings, perhaps we should take a moment to explain them:

Personal	The most successful practices align the aspirations of the clinic with the personal aspirations of the owner(s). It is crucial, therefore, to start with an exploration of what you want personally – so that the practice can be part of delivering it.
Purpose	Once we know your expectations of the practice in the context of your life as a whole, we can start to consider what you want the clinic to achieve. This is important if you are running a clinic on your own, but absolutely crucial if you have staff or associates involved in achieving what you want.
Pipeline	This is the conduit that brings new patients to your practice – a simple concept but a huge topic. As a result, the Pipeline pillar qualifies for two chapters of the book, whereas the others make do with one.
Patients	The central pillar in any successful practice. Without doubt, providing a memorable, positive experience for your patients, and getting them better, is a key part of growing a successful clinic. However, we will show this is so much more than just the treatment.
People	We are some way from computers and robots providing treatments, thank goodness, so the success or otherwise of your clinic will depend on the people within it – you principally, but also your fellow practitioners, your reception and administrative staff, your trusted advisors, subcontractors and many others. This pillar considers how you will manage all of them (including you!).
Profit	We know this is can be an unpopular word amongst practitioners, but it begins with P and maintains our alliteration. Furthermore, we don't want it to be unpopular. Profit is what allows you to live, to feed your kids, to re-invest in the clinic and to have a sustainable presence in your community. So we think profit is a worthy aspiration, and the one important pillar that practitioners often avoid.
Plan	It is our experience that practitioners who have a plan, and who follow and review it, are the ones who find success more consistently. With this pillar, we hope to give you the opportunity to set out your intentions in the short and medium term – so that you can find that success too.

Within each chapter we will be introducing a range of ideas and tips that we hope will get you thinking, then we'll be giving you ways to explore how the tips and ideas apply to you and your clinic specifically. After that, you'll have the chance to relate the outcomes of that work to your overall plan, which can build as you progress through the book. Then all you have to do is implement it...

Implementation seems an appropriate topic with which to close this Introduction. Building a painless practice, whether founded on seven pillars or not, is a process and a journey – not a destination in itself. We do believe that by working through this book you will have a clear map of how to progress from where you are now towards the future you want to create. But when you get there, another future will probably appear as your goal, and another plan will be needed for the next stage. But that's the joy of having your own practice!

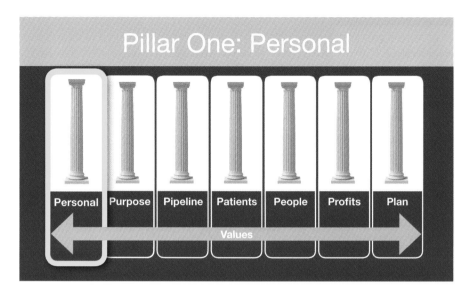

Personal | Purpose | Pipeline | Patients | People | Profits | Plan
Values

Personal

Whether you are just starting out, or you have been running a practice for a while, the chances are you have some idea of what constitutes a successful clinic for you. We explained in the Introduction that we have seen many and various descriptions of success – and they are all correct for the individual concerned. You will, through this chapter, start to define what success means to you.

Before we go too far, however, we need to ensure one thing is very, very clear. It is YOU reading this book, it is YOU who will be working in your practice, and it is YOU who will make it happen. It is therefore totally sensible that we start with, and remember throughout, what YOU want for yourself and YOUR practice. To a degree, nothing else matters. We want to avoid plans based on what you think your parents want, or society expects, or what your college colleagues have implemented. We want a plan that is YOURS. Unless we find that, and why you want it, it is going to be very, very difficult for you to maintain the enthusiasm to finish this book, let alone build a better practice.

The Chesire Cat knew that few people meander their way to true success, and that to get what you want, you must first define it. As Stephen Covey put it, you must begin with

"Would you tell me, please, which way I ought to go from here?"

"That depends a good deal on where you want to get to," said the Cat.

"I don't much care where—" said Alice.

"Then it doesn't matter which way you go," said the Cat.

"—so long as I get somewhere," Alice added as an explanation.

"Oh, you're sure to do that," said the Cat, "if you only walk long enough."

the end in mind. We are going to start exploring what your vision of success might be, and we have a few ways to do that. Our hope is that by the end of this chapter you will have articulated your personal vision, understood why you want that vision, and the role your practice will play in your wider life. We believe that by doing this, your chances of sustained success are enormously improved.

A powerful vision helps define what you will do on a yearly, monthly, weekly and daily basis and, more importantly, it shapes what you won't do. It provides the bigger picture for the detail of your plan. By understanding where you are heading, if you know where you are already, it becomes much easier to plan the route between the two. That may mean you meander less than Alice would, heading somewhere.

Visions are best committed to paper – by writing them out or printing from a computer. This helps the brain process the thoughts and gives you something physical to work from. If the ideas are purely in your mind, they are more susceptible to random thoughts, to doubt and to indecision. Once one's vision is committed to paper, one tends to have greater faith, more resilience and deeper resolve to take the actions required (in our experience).

These exercises can prompt a long series of "yeah buts" where you convince yourself your vision cannot or will not come true. Realism has its place, but do allow yourself to dream. We have had so many experiences where people have given themselves permission to chase seemingly impossible dreams – with amazing results.

Exercise 1: A 70th Birthday

Imagine you are attending the 70th birthday of a loved one – someone you have known for a very long time, someone you hold dear to your heart.

Picture yourself donning your best suit or dress, brushing yourself down, fixing your hair and then driving to the hall for the party. As you arrive, many familiar faces greet you – friends of old, family, people you had forgotten you knew.

Picture the hall, full of balloons, streamers and banners saying 'Happy 70th Birthday'. The guests are milling about, waiting for things to start. Someone rattles a spoon against a cup, coughs and brings the hall to order.

They introduce the order of the day – there will be four short speeches about the guest of honour – one from their family, one from their work or profession, one from the church or community group they have worked with for some time and finally one from one of their closest and longstanding friends. But first, a toast to the 70 year-old! The whole hall stands and raises their glass – to you!

If you could stand now at your 70th birthday party, what would you want said in those four speeches? Think hard and deep. What kind of a father, mother, wife, husband, or sibling would you want them to say you were? How would you like your peers to describe your contribution to your work? What of those friends, how might they recount the years?

What difference would you like to have made in your guests lives? Jot down the bullet points from each speech.

Family
-
-
-
-
-

Community
-
-
-
-
-

Work
-
-
-
-
-

Friends
-
-
-
-
-

Exercise 2: 2020 Vision

For your second exercise, we want you to think of a significant date in the future, somewhere between 5 and 10 years distant – this may be a general date like 1 Jan 2020, or it may be personal to you like your 30th, 40th, 60th birthday etc. The key thing is to have the long, but not too long, timescale of between 5 and 10 years.

From the perspective of that milestone, list what you want to be true, in terms of your achievements, on that date. To help you get started, here are some suggested topics to consider:

Career (your work) – what would you want to have achieved in your career? What sort of practice do you want to create? What level do you want to have reached within your profession?

Community (your village or town, interest groups, religious body, friends or wider family) – what would you want in terms of your connections with that community? For example, some people want to be active in their village, or to be working with a charity related to a personal cause, or they want to be part of a church congregation.

Education (what you will have learnt) – what exams do you want to pass, what other things do you want to learn? For some this is a Masters in their field, for others it is to learn a language, or to obtain a pilot's licence.

Environment (your surroundings, not the global climate) – what sort of house would you like to live in, where will it be, do you want the lounge finally decorated? For example, James has on his list a house with a stream or river in the garden.

Experiences – what do you want to have done? This may be a bungee or parachute jump, sailing the world, attending Wimbledon, seeing an opera, spending a year in New Zealand, whatever excites you.

Finance (your personal finances) – how much would you like to pay off your debt or save for the future, or be earning each year, or be spending each year?

Health (your personal wellbeing) – very few people write down "I want to be ill", but how do you define health? Do you want to gain weight/lose weight, be able to play football with the kids, give up smoking, get your eyesight corrected? One client wrote "to be able to run a mile without dying" (and now regularly runs six mile races!).

Relationships (with your spouse/significant other, children, parents or siblings) – what do you want to be true about these relationships? Do you want to find a spouse, leave a spouse, be a good parent, re-establish a relationship with a sibling?

Legacy – what do you want to leave behind? This may be financial, it may be charitable, it could be well-adjusted, functioning offspring. It may be a legacy in the awareness and well-being you have brought to patients. It may be all of these.

Use this worksheet to set out your vision for your milestone date.

On this date .... I want this to be true.

Career
-
-
-
-

Community
-
-
-
-

Education
-
-
-
-

Environment
-
-
-
-

Experience
-
-
-
-

Finance
-
-
-
-

Health
-
-
-
-

Relationships
-
-
-
-

Legacy
-
-
-
-

Once you have these desired achievements listed, you can start to see how they interrelate (you may wish to do your year travelling in Nepal before you have children, for example). You can also start to break them down into what needs to happen for them to come true, and what you need to be doing now. For example, if a finance goal was to save an additional £50 a month, you could choose to forego your daily take-out coffee at £2.50, saving the required amount each month. A long term goal has been broken down to a daily action.

Exercise 3: Clarifying your Values

Before we further polish your personal vision, we need to understand more about what motivates you on a personal level. It is likely that there are certain things that drive you: core things that, whatever the situation, you will be true to. These are what we term your values. Not values in the sense of moral standards, but values as in what you truly value in life. They are part of the solid centre we come back to in times of uncertainty, indecision or challenge. When we express those values in our work and other actions, we are motivated, energised and productive. When we are not expressing them, or are in conflict with them, we are de-motivated, lethargic and uninspired.

The purpose of this exercise is to find those things that do motivate you, that will make you bounce out of bed in the morning, which will give you resolve to overcome setbacks and keep working towards your vision.

On the next page is a list of words – read through the list and think which words most appeal to you. Ring those words and then transfer them to the table at the bottom. As you do so, look to see if they fall into groups (they often do). Group the words as you write them down in the six boxes provided. If you can think of other words that inspire you, which are not listed, just add them.

Find a word to summarise each group (it may be one of those there, or another word). That word is likely to be one of your core values. Try to distil your initials words into up to six groups (with one word summing up each group).

You should now have up to six words that summarise your true values (and will probably summarise the values of your practice).

Possible Business or Personal Values:

Accomplish	Enhance	Ingenuity	Reliable
Acquire	Enjoy	Innovate	Respected
Assemble	Enlighten	Instruct	Responsive
Attractive	Ethical	Integrated	Risk
Automated	Excellence	Invent	Serve
Best	Exclusive	In touch with	Speculation
Budget	Expensive	Joyful	Spiritual
Care	Experiment	Knowledge	Stimulate
Catalyse	Explain	Learn	Sufficient
Change	Facilitate	Linked	Support
Collaborative	First	Local	Teach
Community	Foster	Modern	Technological
Contribute	Fun	Nurture	Thrill
Control	Gamble	Open	Timely
Cost-effective	Gentle	Originality	Traditional
Create	Grace	Partnership	Treat
Cutting Edge	Grant	Passion	Trustworthy
Danger	Greatest	Personal	Unconventional
Design	Global	Plan	Unique
Develop	Historic	Play	Value
Discover	Honest	Practical	Yearn
Dominate	Impact	Produce	Youthful
Empathise	Improve	Professional	Zany
Endeavour	Independence	Quality	Zealous

Pulling it together

You will now have completed three exercises which are quite introspective and reflective. This should have helped you develop your picture of what you want from your life overall, and the role your practice is going to play in that. The three exercises are designed to bring out different aspects: the first two look at WHERE you want to get to and the third exercise should help you see a bit more of HOW you want to get there, providing you with guidelines to refer to along your journey.

It is our belief that one's business or practice is not a destination in itself – but it is the vehicle which will take you to a destination. It is very rare for someone to want to create a clinic purely for the purpose of creating a clinic – usually the clinic meets some other need(s). If we conceive of the practice as your vehicle to a destination of your choice, the joy of having your own business is that you have much greater freedom in choosing the nature of your vehicle. You can decide the hours of work, the feel of the practice, the financial model and so much more.

One important consideration will be location – you may want it close to (or at) home to limit your travelling. You may want it near your existing family base – which may be where you have grown up, or where you have settled with a spouse. It may be near the location of your leisure pursuits. All of these are valid criteria for choosing a location. In the Pipeline Pillar we will consider some market-based factors you need to consider too.

What type of vehicle do you want?

When choosing a car, we will often have a list of criteria that determine the brand and model we end up with. That is what stops us buying a two-seater convertible when we need a family car for the kids. You should, by now, be starting to develop a list of criteria of what you want from your practice, when it is successful, to deliver your vision. As the business owner, you get to choose. Don't believe the myth that a business owner has to work long hours, do all the work and take no reward.

Things you may wish to consider:

- How many days a week do you want to work, and what hours?
- What does your ideal day look like?
- How does your practice integrate with your other commitments?
- How much holiday will you take?
- What career breaks are you planning, if any?
- How much do you want to be earning?
- Are you happy managing people, or do you want to stay on your own?
- Will you have one site, or more than one?
- Will you have other therapies in your practice?

- What sort?

- How big do you want your practice to be?

- Will you specialise in particular interests?

- What values will underpin your practice?

- How will it look?

- Who will be on your team?

The answers to each of these questions, and others you feel are relevant, will start to define your choices. Each answer will have implications – if you want to work at home on your own, that will probably have implications for how much you will earn from the business. If you have a team, the earnings could be extended (it could also go down, but we'll explain how to avoid that in the Profit Pillar).

It is probable that you will want or need to discuss your evolving plans with significant people in your life – especially spouses. If you want a year in Fiji, and they think a week in Brighton is an adventure, you're going to need to talk. You may find your plans go through a couple of iterations as you discuss it with others and then reflect.

When you feel you are getting to a vision that really fires you up, turn to page 110 and start filling in the first sections of your plan.

Summary of Pillar 1: Personal

- This is your practice, so you get to decide how it looks, what it does and why it does it.

- That decision is best made within the context of your overall plan for your life.

- You can create that plan by considering what you want to achieve by a certain date, and by what you would want those close to you to say about you in your old age.

- To achieve success, you need to know what that success is – what it looks, smells, sounds and feels like.

- A vision that is committed to paper has had greater analysis and is less prone to buffeting and change by random factors.

- Your personal values are what will motivate you on good days and bad – ensuring you use these as criteria when choosing a path forward will increase the chances you will be successful.

- The location of your practice is part of your overall personal plan. Subject to certain market criteria, you can choose what will work for you in a wider context.

- Your business/practice is the vehicle to take you to your destination, not an end in itself. You get to decide what that vehicle will be like.

- The model of practice you choose will have implications for how far and how fast you can travel – you need to ensure your vehicle is the right type to get you to your destination.

- Your vision will probably benefit from discussion with other key stakeholders – especially spouses. You will iterate the vision as you work through the inter-relations between different facets of your dreams.

- Now we have the end in mind, we can begin to make it a reality!

Key Learning Outcomes from this Chapter:

I have realised:

-
-
-
-
-

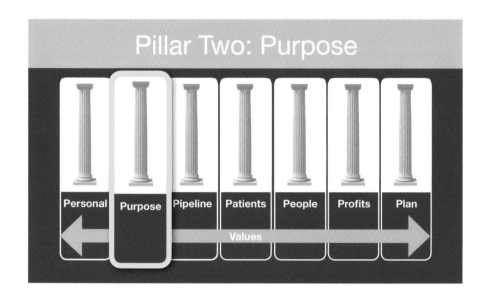

Purpose

It is said that a visitor to a NASA site in the late 1960s stopped and asked a janitor, who was sweeping up in a research building, what his reason for working there was. "I'm putting a man on the moon" was his reply. If true, this is the epitome of a business purpose permeating every layer of an organisation. Mission Statements and Visions receive a cynical and sceptical reaction amongst many employees, but when done well and with integrity they can spur teams on to achieve beyond their expectations.

Whether you are going to be working on your own, or as part of a team, it is important to understand why you are doing it. The last chapter will have given you an idea of your personal motivations for wanting to treat patients and in what type of clinic. Your purpose builds on this, and allows you to communicate it to others and to inspire them to help you make it happen – whether they are colleagues, patients, the bank, or suppliers.

Exercise 4: Practice Purpose

In the space below, write out the purpose of your clinic – why does it exist, and what does it aim to do? The intention of giving you limited space is to help you be brief!

....

....

If you want some help with a few ideas, our purpose at Painless Practice is:

> *To see every practice owner*
> *enjoying their work*
> *and achieving their vision.*

The high-wire forest adventure company Go Ape have a business purpose that we love:

> *To create adventure*
> *and encourage everyone*
> *to live life adventurously.*

Tristram Mayhew, who runs Go Ape, will tell you that this ethos underpins their decision-making daily – from big strategic considerations to individual customer interactions. We would hope the same is true of Painless Practice and our work. What about something for a practitioner's practice? A workshop participant created the following (the Minehead bit is made up, to preserve anonymity):

> *Bringing a better quality of life*
> *to the people of Minehead*
> *through pain relief, improved mobility*
> *and health education.*

We liked this example because it specifies their customers (the people of Minehead – not the dogs or cats, and not the whole of the West Country), and it specifies the benefits they bring, not the therapy. If the purpose is to "provide chiropractic in Minehead", for example, it limits your intention to just one intervention: what if chiropractic is not the most appropriate treatment for the patient? Conversely, by not specifying people, it opens up the possibility of treating animals – which may be what you want, but should be avoided if it isn't what you want.

So, what's yours? When you have played with it a bit, and are happy with it, you can add it to the relevant part of your Plan on page 111.

A clear understanding of the purpose of the business or clinic is usually a helpful step, but it is not the whole journey. The next step is to take this down a level and consider what your objectives are in the medium to long term. This may be numerical (provide 100 treatments a week) or it may be a wider aspiration (be known as the best complementary health centre in Minehead). In fact you may have a number of objectives which could include both examples above, and others.

In order for you to achieve your purpose, what objectives do you need to set? For example, Painless Practice wants to see every practice owner enjoying their work and achieving their vision. What objectives would support that? We realise we'll probably be doing this one owner at a time, so we have objectives to get the word out there that it is possible to enjoy your work and achieve your vision (this book, our speaking engagements, other communications). We then have further objectives for the number of workshops we want to deliver, how many participants will attend, how many clients we will have in a year and so on.

This idea of objectives below the purpose can be shown in the Pyramid of Goals.

Source: After Burke et al, Growing Your Business, 2008.

You defined your personal goals in the last chapter, decided upon your practice purpose earlier and have now started setting Objectives that will fulfil both the Goals and the Purpose. The Tasks and Actions will come as you work through the chapters and fill out the plan.

Exercise 5: Setting Objectives

Use the worksheet below to set out the objectives you can already see will be part of your clinic's success. Try to define success as clearly as possible – with a date. In this way you will know you have achieved your objective and whether you have achieved it on time. Once you have played with these, they can be transferred to page 111 as part of your Plan.

Note: *It may be that some of the objectives cannot be inserted until after you have done some work on the other chapters – especially the Pipeline, People and Profit Pillars. In that case, leave them now but remember to come back to them.*

Question	Your answer	Target Date
How would you describe the nature of your clinic (eg small, multi-disciplinary, at home, in a gym)?		
How many practitioners do you expect to have? How many staff to support you?		
How many treatments will the clinic provide in a week, month or year?		
How many new patients will you want in a week, month and year?		
How much do you want to earn (profit) from the clinic?		
What sort of reputation do you want in the community?		
How many premises will you have – just one, or a chain?		
What sort of patient outcomes do you want – what % of patients should expect to get better?		
What other objectives do you have?		

Note: *You may wish to set a series of targets – building up to a five year plan. For example patient numbers may be 10/wk in Year 1, 25/wk in Year 2 and 40/wk in Year 3.*

Summary of Pillar 2: Purpose

- It is important to understand why you want to run a practice (what is its purpose?).

- A practice's purpose is more effective when relatively brief, and where the market and service are defined.

- Your Personal Goals will shape the Purpose for the practice.

- Both your Personal Goals and the Purpose will define your Objectives.

- Objectives usually contain a numerical measure of success and a target date.

- Your Objectives are likely to be refined as you work through this book – so we suggest you leave room for more to be added!

- With your Personal Goals, Practice Purpose and Objectives in your plan, it is time to start considering how you will market the clinic and get people ringing for appointments.

Key Learning Outcomes from this Chapter:

I have realised:

-

-

-

-

-

-

-

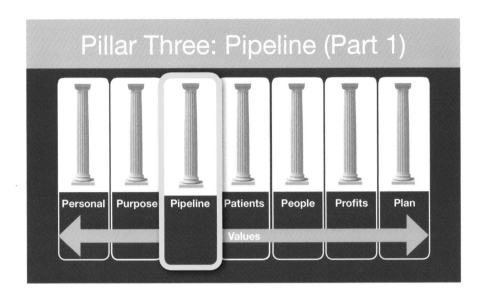

Pipeline (Part 1)

As we said in the Introduction, the Pipeline is the pillar about which we are asked the most, and about which we probably have the most to say. Marketing a clinic is an enormous topic, and there are so many tips we could share to help you grow the practice you want. However, the essence of successful marketing is focus – and we will attempt to model that in the next two chapters. As we take you through the many elements of creating a successful pipeline, your task will be to sift out those elements that are most pertinent to you.

First, let's explain the concept of a pipeline. This is a metaphor often used in a sales environment in business, because it is easily understood. For any business or practice to thrive, it needs a steady flow of new customers/patients through the front door. Your sales and marketing pipeline is the device that delivers those new patients to the door. In this chapter, we will consider the many factors that are important in getting people into the pipeline. In the following chapter, we will also talk about how to manage that pipeline so that new patients drop out the bottom and knock on the door.

Understand Your Territory

You now have a picture of what it is that you want to achieve with your therapy career (your personal goals and your purpose) and why that is important to you (your values). We are now going to bring that theoretical plan into the hard reality of the marketplace and consider where you will be located.

Larger companies will build a business case when deciding where to open new premises, by considering a range of issues:

Demographic factors:

- Rural versus urban

- Income distribution

- Age profiles

- Areas of consumer spend

- Distance travelled to access services

- Key employers (companies and industries)

Market factors:

- Levels of demand

- Affordability of service

- Knowledge and acceptance of service

- Potential high-demand areas

- Direct and indirect competition

For a clinic, the same factors need to be considered, but the personal criteria and goals we discussed in the Purpose Pillar are likely to hold more sway. However, you will need to ensure your personal goals are consistent with the market factors. If you want to live in the Outer Hebrides, you may not be able to create a clinic providing 3000 treatments a month.

Exercise 6: Understand Your Territory

Answer the following questions about your location, to determine its suitability for the sort of practice you are planning:

Describe the nature of the community where you will be based:

- Is it rural, urban or semi-urban?

- What is the resident population of the community?

- What is the resident population within reasonable driving time?

- What level of seasonal or daily increase/decrease in population is there (because of tourists, commuters etc)?

- What is the income distribution of the community – is it low income, middle or affluent?

- What is the age profile of the population – are there significantly more young families, or older people, for example?

- What trends are likely to affect population and age or income distribution? Are large developments planned, is the population aging or are young people moving in?

- Who are the key employers in the area – any large factories or offices?

- What sectors are most local people employed in?

- What awareness and demand already exists for the service you plan to provide?

- What other providers are in the area – of your therapy and of other therapies that patients might choose instead of visiting you?

- What locally may give rise to particular demand – eg sports clubs or retirement homes?

- Given local income levels, and the prices charged by other providers, what is likely to be the price point for your service?

Go to page 112 to complete your plan – 'description of the local market place'

These questions will help you consider the factors relating to where you want to set up your practice. You will need to do some research to answer the questions – your local authority is usually a good source of some of the statistics, or the Neighbourhood Statistics section of the Office for National Statistics website (www.neighbourhood.statistics.gov.uk). Some information you will build by knowing the area – such as local employers etc. If the area is new to you, chat to a few people to get a feel for the area.

If you already have a practice running, we would hazard a guess that you didn't put in the work to do this research when you opened – you will still get benefit from doing the exercise now.

Your Specific Location

The analysis above will have allowed you to decide upon the general geographic area in which you want to practice – perhaps a neighbourhood in a city, or a part of a town or a village. The next level is to consider a specific location – thinking about which criteria you will be using when choosing a site. We are assuming here that you are only having one clinic. If you plan more, you can just repeat the exercise for each location, being careful to not cannibalise the market of one clinic by opening another too close.

You will now need to consider:

- Cost of purchase/rent and business rates

- Opportunity – what premises are actually available?

- What type of location will be consistent with the type of practice you want (see the discussion about brand on the next page)?

- Do you want a prominent, visible location?

- What parking will you want, or will proximity to public transport be more important?

- What access requirements will you have – no steps on entry, treatment rooms all on one floor, etc?

- Will these premises be a stepping stone, or a long-term project?

- Would it be better to buy or rent?

- What planning issues may relate to your site?

- What size will meet your short-to-medium term needs, what expansion opportunities will you need?

We should also stress that all of the above questions apply equally to a practice in your home, as well as a commercial premises.

Exercise 7: Location, Location, Location

Write out the key characteristics of your ideal location – both in terms of neighbourhood and specific site. If you are still looking for a site, you could use this to sketch on a local map where potentials sites will be, and use this to guide discussions with property agents. If you already have a site, evaluate whether it meets your needs. If you cannot move, consider what things you could do to your current location to make it more like your ideal location.

Transfer the outcome of this thought process to the key features section of your Plan (page 112).

Unique Selling Proposition and Brand

In most marketing textbooks you will find lengthy discussion of these concepts, with good reason as they are fundamental to the theory and practice of successful marketing. So we will explain them here, and consider how they apply to your practice:

Unique Selling Proposition (USP): The thing about your practice and you that makes you different from all the other choices a potential patient has (not just what makes you different from others offering the same therapy).

Brand: The reputation and image that you and your practice have amongst patients and the wider community. This includes, but is much, much wider than, the name of the practice or your logo. This reputation is in the minds of the community you seek to serve – whether you cultivate and influence it or not.

We often hear that terms like this are not relevant to small businesses, especially those in the health sector. We beg to differ. Your USP is the answer to the simple question "why you?" and if you are unable to articulate a response, you will make it harder for yourself to attract patients.

Exercise 8: Deciding your USP

Complete the following sentence (ideally in the space provided to keep it succinct!):

Patients will come to... <insert clinic name*> because

....

....

....

....

*See the comments about choosing your clinic name on the following page.

We should just add that clichés like "good customer service" or "high quality" rarely make you unique – do you know a practitioner who proclaims that they provide low quality care and poor customer service? When you have clarified your USP, you can add it to your Plan on page 113.

Whether intentionally or not, we all create an emotional reaction in others when they think of us – this is true on a personal level, but is especially true on a business level. Think about your local paper shop, your local supermarket, your local mechanic and your local pub. Each of those will generate some sort of positive or negative, warm or cold, loyal or disinterested reaction, and yet it is probably only the supermarket that we would traditionally consider had a brand.

To illustrate the point, consider the brand Polo. If we consider the Volkswagen Polo, we might think German engineering, reliability and solidity. If we thought of Polo by Ralph Lauren, we might think of quality fashion, or over-priced designer labels. If we thought of the mint with the hole, we might smile, remembering eating them as a child, we probably feel warm towards the brand. Polo – same word, probably three different emotional reactions, depending on the brand associated with it.

As a practitioner you are unlikely to have the marketing budget of Volkswagen, Ralph Lauren or Nestlé but there is still a lot you can do to influence how your community reacts to your brand. Factors that will affect that emotional reaction include, amongst other things:

- The name you choose
- The colours and fonts you deploy in your marketing, communications and signage
- The style and quality of your marketing
- The type of building you locate in – a gym, a log cabin, or an industrial unit convey different things
- The colour, quality and freshness of decor in the practice
- The manner in which the phone is answered, or patients are welcomed into the practice
- The form of clothing worn by all those working in the practice
- The attention to detail, such as timekeeping, that you routinely show

We mentioned the name of the practice in the points above. To some degree, the words don't really matter – we have shown how different a brand can be even using the word Polo. However, if the neighbourhood you intend to practice in is Badback, or your surname is Quack you might want to think twice. We know a practitioner whose surname is Hussey, and didn't hesitate to use their surname in their practice name. Yet every time we get workshop audiences to critique their marketing materials, people cannot believe they used that name.

Similarly, if you name the clinic after yourself, what implications will that have if you want to treat less, or sell the clinic? If you name it after the road you first practice in, what happens if you move? In the era of Google and search engines, having your town name in your name can help (if you buy the relevant website domain) – but what happens if you want to open a second clinic? You need to think these issues through, but not get too hung up on it. Messrs Marks, Spencer or Sainsbury no longer work in their stores, and it doesn't seem to matter. Norwich Union, Halifax and Lakeland Plastics have all outgrown their geographic roots.

We could not leave the topic of branding without one other suggestion. As you build your practice, and probably early on, you may want to protect your brand by registering a trademark with the Intellectual Property Office (www.ipo.gov.uk). They can advise on whether your name can be trademarked and the whole process costs a few hundred pounds – but can prevent many problems in the future.

Exercise 9: Your Brand

Write out the words you would want your market to use to describe their reaction to your brand. You may find that your values from Exercise 3 are a place to start, but you will probably have other words. Come up with a clear idea of what brand you want to establish – so when we get to talking about the design and style of your marketing, you have a clear idea of what you want to establish. Once you have the essence of your brand, you can complete that section in the Plan (page 113).

Marketing Mix

A third key concept in marketing theory is the marketing mix. Traditionally this is based on four Ps (different to our Seven Pillars!):

Price	Price is one of the ways in which service providers establish themselves in the market. Lower price often implies lower quality, whilst higher prices can restrict the market and imply better service or greater exclusivity.
Product	In your context, this is the service you provide. Most practitioners will conceive this as their particular profession – eg osteopathy or chiropractic. In truth, the patient probably perceives the product differently – as pain relief, improved mobility, faster return to work etc. You may do better by thinking and talking in terms of patient benefits, not the features of your therapy.
Promotion	This is the marketing support you provide for your service – where will people learn about what you can do for them, and why they should come to you? What offers might you make to entice them in?
Placement	This covers how people can access your service. Most obviously this will include the location and accessibility of your clinic, but you may also provide home visits, or regular "surgeries" in large local employers.

As you develop your plans for marketing your clinic, you will need to consider the four Ps of the marketing mix to ensure you get the balance right.

Now might be a good time to talk about pricing. In our experience, practitioners generally charge too little for their services, and rarely put their prices up. We will talk more about this in the Profit pillar, but here we will mention the importance of pricing in the marketing mix.

We know a practitioner who is deliberately the dearest in his city. As a result, he attracts patients who think he must be the best in the city. Other practitioners price themselves below a hairdresser – and then struggle to establish commitment and a perception of professionalism from their patients. We encounter many practitioners who have altruistic concerns that some patients may not then be able to afford their services. At the margin, it is possible that this is true, but why charge everyone else less to compensate? If you believe a potential patient genuinely cannot afford treatment, you could consider discounting just for them. 'Genuinely' is key here, we know of a practitioner who had been providing treatments at a concessionary rate only to see his client arriving in a brand new luxury car one day

Patient Sources

For most practitioners, almost anyone is a possible patient. This is great in that you have a wide potential market, but a disaster in that you can easily lose focus in your marketing. By narrowing your attention down to some specific areas you can probably have greater impact. The intention is not to find thousands of sources, because that would be overwhelming, but to identify enough for you to work on energetically and consistently. Focus is as important as creativity.

Potential Sources of Patients

Personal Referrals	Direct
• Word of Mouth • Returning Patients • Friends/Family • Leisure Contacts	• Respond to Advertising • Web Search/ Google Ads • Walk-in from street • Read PR
Sports • Rugby • Athletics • Football • Golf • Tennis	**Business Connections** • Networking Groups • Large Employers • Local Authorities • Strategic Alliances • Retailers
Interest Groups • Women's Institute • National Childbirth Trust • Senior Citizen's Groups • Patient Support Groups	**Clinical Referrals** • GP Practices • Insurance Companies • Other Practitioners

Note: By Strategic Alliances we mean a commercial link with someone like a gym, health club, spa or local employer. By Retailers we mean shops also selling to your target market – such as shoe shops, running shops, bed shops or hairdressers.

In our view, every practice should focus most on those in the top left box – because this is the most fertile soil for growing a practice. You will then need to choose a handful of the sources listed in the other boxes to focus on – and then decide the specific actions you will take to attract patients from those sources (choose the sources now, consider the actions after you have read the next chapter).

Exercise 10: Your Key Patient Sources

Read through the table opposite and decide which of the patient sources are likely to be most relevant to your market and of most interest to you. We will start you with those in the top left box – which others will you add?

My Patient Sources:

- Word of Mouth
- Friends/Family
-
-
-
-

- Returning Patients
- Leisure Contacts
-
-
-
-

These target areas can then be transferred to your Plan (page 114). We sometimes get resistance to the idea of narrowing the focus to just a few sources. People don't want to 'miss out' on patients from the other options. We are not suggesting that if you do not choose GP practices as a source to focus on, you should turn away any patients that come from a GP. Welcome patients from any source! We are merely suggesting that your marketing will be more effective if you focus your resources of time, energy and money in specific areas. Consider a grizzly bear in the wilds of Canada in September. He is at the top of the food chain, and can eat pretty much anything he likes. If he finds an ant hill, he can force his way into it and eat all the tiny ants. But he also knows if he stands in the river, in the right spot, migrating salmon will jump down his throat. Where should he focus?

Perfect Patients

For many years we have been recommending Attracting Perfect Customers (by Stacey Hall and Jan Brogniez – see Reading List, page 127) to our clients. We repeatedly found they had amazing results from using it – so much so that we thought we should read it and apply it to Painless Practice. We have never looked back. We would love for you to have Perfect Patients, and we invite you to complete this exercise and see what happens.

Exercise 11: My Perfect Patient

Find a quiet place where you will be free from disturbance, and focus yourself on the exercise at hand. If you already have a practice, think through the patients that are what you would call perfect – the ones you enjoy treating, the ones who are good for the clinic, and so on. If you have yet to start, try to imagine who they would be.

Set out the qualities that your perfect patients show using the worksheet on the following page. It doesn't matter if no individual patient currently shows all of the qualities. Next consider what you will need to do to attract those perfect patients. Hall and Brogniez have a more detailed process with further questions, which we have found works, so you if this idea interests you, we recommend you get their book and work through it.

As you might expect by now, there is space in your Plan to enter the qualities of your Perfect Patient, and how you will attract them. (page 114).

If you have others working with you – associates, receptionists, practice managers, other practitioners in your building – you may wish to conduct this exercise with them, to engage them in your process, and to hear their thoughts to add to yours.

My Perfect Patient

The qualities that make my patients perfect are:

-
-
-
-
-
-
-
-
-
-
-
-

To attract those perfect patients I will need to:

-
-
-
-
-
-
-
-
-
-
-
-

Summary of Pillar 3: Pipeline (Part 1)

- You will need to consider a number of demographic and socioeconomic factors when choosing the location of your practice(s).

- Market factors such as the level of demand and local competition will also need to be considered.

- To choose a specific premises, you will need to balance costs against factors such as access to public transport or parking, prominence, size and ambience.

- Your Unique Selling Proposition will establish why potential patients will choose your practice over other options – it is important that you know what it is and can articulate it.

- Your brand is how you are perceived by your community – many factors will determine that perception and it is your job to manage and influence it.

- Your choice of name for the practice is only part of the brand, but your choice may have wider implications.

- As your brand becomes established, it may well be prudent to protect it by registering a trademark.

- Price is an important part of your marketing mix – too low a price can send the wrong message, as well as limiting your earning potential.

- Your patients will come from a range of sources. Personal referrals are likely to be the most fertile source.

- So that you don't rely solely on referrals (especially when you start and have no or few patients to refer to you), you will want five or six other sources that you can focus on.

- If you define what makes your Perfect Patient, and reflect regularly on what makes them perfect and how you might attract them, there is a school of thought (which we subscribe to) that you WILL attract them.

Key Learning Outcomes from this Chapter:

I have realised:

-
-
-
-
-

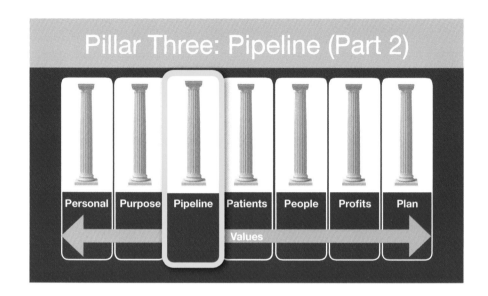

Personal | Purpose | Pipeline | Patients | People | Profits | Plan

Values

Pipeline (Part 2)

Let us take stock of where we hope you are now. You have articulated your own Personal Goals and drivers, and the Purpose behind setting up (or continuing to run) your practice. You have started to set high-level objectives that will enable you to fulfil that Purpose, and achieve your Personal goals. In the last chapter we started to consider the vast area of how to market your practice, in order to achieve those objectives. If you have been doing the exercises, and transferring the outcomes to the relevant sections, your Plan will be starting to come together.

We now want to turn your attention to some of the mechanics of the Pipeline – what to actually do, and how, in order to get the phone ringing with new patients. Towards the end of the last chapter we talked about Attracting Perfect Customers, and we do believe that attraction is the best way to gain new patients. However, we also believe that unless the people out there know how attractive you are, you're not going to pull them in. So, this chapter considers how you might transmit that attractiveness – like a songbird singing to attract a mate.

The objectives you created earlier (Exercise 5 on Page 26, or page 111 of your Plan) should give you an idea of what outcome you want from your marketing activities (eg 10 New Patients a week). Using the idea of a pipeline allows you to plan what activity you need to undertake. Consider the diagram overleaf.

In this stylised version of a pipeline for practitioners, we have a 4–stage process. A proportion of enquiries to the practice become new patient consultations. A proportion of those become a treated patient (they complete a course of treatment).

A yet smaller proportion of those come back for treatment of other episodes, or for maintenance, and become a returning patient. (We accept that for some therapies there is no concept of returning patients – it is almost unheard of for them to treat the same person twice. Their pipeline will be one stage shorter.)

We could start to apply some numbers to these proportions:

	Conversion Ratio	Number required to generate 1 person at end of pipe
Enquiries	60%	10
New Patient Consultation	66%	6
Treated Patient	25%	4
Regular, Returning Patient	n/a	1

So, in this example, of every ten people who call the practice, 60% will book and attend a new patient consultation. Of those six, 66% will complete their treatment cycle (usually more than one treatment for most practitioners, but not all). Of those four, 25% will come back in the future for regular treatment or for other episodic interventions.

If our intention is to increase the number of people at the end of that pipe (regular, returning patients), we can do two things: improve the conversion ratios down the pipe, so that more of the ten get to the end; or pour more enquiries into the first stage of the pipe. Typically, people in small business, including practitioners, focus on the latter and neglect the former. In our experience, dealing with both is the most productive. We will consider improving the ratios in the Patients Pillar, and here we consider how to pour more enquiries into the pipe.

In our pipeline example, we know that ten enquiries will generate six new patient consultations. If we want ten new patients a week, we will need to generate seventeen enquiries a week. We can build that up from a range of sources – for example:

Referrals	8	47%
Google	4	23%
Walk Ins (see signs)	2	12%
Link with gym nearby	2	12%
GP referral	1	6%
Total	17	

We can then start to plan what activity we need to undertake to generate this level of enquiries from these sources – and your marketing plan will start to form.

Exercise 12: Patient Sources

Refer back to the Objectives you started to set out in Exercise 5 (page 26) and have already entered in your Plan (page 111). Use this pipeline worksheet to estimate your own conversion ratios, and thus what average level of enquiries you will need to generate.

What conversion ratios and numbers would you enter for your pipeline?

	Conversion Ratio	Number required to generate 1 person at end of pipe
Enquiries	%	
New Patient Consultation	%	
Treated Patient	%	
Regular, Returning Patient	n/a	

I expect to generate that level of enquiries from the following key sources:

-
-
-
-
-
-

If your own pipeline has more or different stages, you can use this blank template below:

	Conversion Ratio	Number required to generate 1 person at end of pipe
	%	
	%	
	%	
	n/a	

I expect to generate that level of enquiries from the following key sources:

-
-
-
-
-
-

Once you are happy with the numbers, you can transfer them to the relevant part of your Plan (page 114).

Strategies and Tactics

Now perhaps we should consider what strategies and tactics might generate these referrals. We believe there are six broad strategies that you can use to attract new patients:

- Direct Contact/Follow Up
- Networking/Getting Referrals
- Public Speaking
- Writing/Publicity
- Promotional Events
- Advertising

A mix of specific tactics across these various strategies usually makes a good plan, and the precise blend for you will depend on your skills, abilities and resources. For example, it is possible to broadly generalise that the different strategies have different implications along the following lines:

Strategy	Amount of Time	Cost	Effectiveness	Active/ Passive
Direct Contact	Highest	Lowest	Highest	Most Active
Networking	Higher	Lower	Higher	Higher
Public Speaking	Medium	Medium	Medium	Medium
Writing/ Publicity	Medium	Medium	Medium	Medium
Promotional Events	Lower	Higher	Lower	Lower
Advertising	Lowest	Highest	Lowest	Least Active (Most Passive)

The implications are an important consideration – because the strategies you choose will be affected by the availability of time and money in particular. Start-ups are usually time rich and cash poor, so you may want to favour strategies that take time but are lower cost. Conversely, if you are an established practice and you are busy treating a lot of patients during the week, you may be time poor but may have better cashflow. In that situation you could consider less time-intensive strategies, but which may carry more expense.

Before we go too much further, it is probably appropriate to set out what specific tactics you could use within each strategy, then you can start to consider what would be appropriate for you. At various workshops around the country we have asked established and trainee practitioners to generate lists of possible marketing activities.

As one might expect, the students tend to be less conventional, more inventive and in some cases quite alarming – we have only included the legal and less offensive ones here!

Strategy – Advertising *(most passive first)*	
Tactic	**Notes**
Local newspapers	Helps develop presence in a community, but can be expensive. Always best to negotiate and have a series of ads, not a one-off. Ask for a column or editorial too.
Yellow Pages	Declining rapidly as a source of patients. Consider size and look of ad carefully – don't always trust the salesman's statistics. Does your professional association have a corporate ad?
Local directories	Like Yellow Pages, but more localised distribution.
Village newsletters	Shows greater link with local community. People seem to trust ads in these more than ads in newspapers.
Yell.com etc	The internet is steadily replacing print media – paid directory listings are part of that advertising mix, but can be expensive per enquiry generated.
Direct mail	Has low average response rates and can be expensive, but some practitioners have used it to good effect. Design and targeted distribution is crucial.
Flyers	Can be effective if left in sight of target markets (through referral partners). Optimise quality of design and print within your budget. Less effective if printed and then stored in your garage (as seems the norm!).
Bulletin board posters	Can be effective in workplaces, surgeries etc. Best results seem to come where you have a connection with that location already.
Town/estate agents maps	Can be expensive and we have heard no stories of this being beneficial to anyone other than the ad sales guy.
Professional associations' online directories	Why wouldn't you be listed? Make as much of the listing as possible – stand out from all the basic listings.

Regulator's directory	If you have a statutory register, you will probably be listed. Do what you can to have more than a basic listing – anything to get people choosing you over others.
Google Ads	A less expensive way of advertising, in a growing media. Statistics show that fewer and fewer people look at Google Ads, but some practitioners get great returns. Should only be used alongside optimisation of your actual website.
Your own website	Most practitioners' websites are online adverts – and that is fine. But a stunning billboard serves no purpose if no-one finds it. Spend as much on optimising your site (and getting traffic) as you do on making it pretty.

Strategy – Promotional Events

Free assessments	Can create interest and build credibility. Spinal checks work brilliantly for many chiropractors. Will get you noticed and get people talking about you. Be careful to not give too much away on the free assessment.
Open days/evenings	Builds a relationship with patients and referral sources. Can increase their commitment to your success. Very good when tied in with opening/ expanding/redecorating/ summer/winter/oh, who needs an excuse!
Discounts	Short term promotions can create a stimulus to take action, and can create a greater perception of value. However, they can attract purely bargain-seekers, and can undermine the perception of value you are trying to create. We advise long consideration before using discounts.
Groupon etc offers	A growing phenomenon, particularly in cities. Companies offer discounts to a company who then email a membership list. Very popular with restaurants, also used by practitioners. Some professions have issues with their regulator in this area – so always check.
Office visits	If you can be portable, why not take yourself to the patients? We know of practitioners who successfully set up a mobile practice in large office buildings

	or other employers. This may be where a special discount at the launch of a service would work.
Reduced fee for maintenance visits	If you build a practice around maintenance programmes, you could discount those attending regularly, like a loyalty reward. You won't want to create dependence, but you can become part of a patient's regular support team – like their dentist or optician.
Roadshows	This will get you out of the practice and in front of new people in your community – will need careful planning, but will extend your reach.
Tradeshows	Health fairs are becoming increasingly common – could you take a slot at one of those?
Events	We know practitioners who have provided treatments at major golf tournaments, or after local 10K runs. This could be a great PR opportunity.
Service packages	You could work with strategic partners to offer a bundle of services – linking with spa days for women, activity days for employers, promoting orthopaedic mattresses etc
National promotions	Every day or week seems to be some sort of special day – Back Care Week, Alzheimer's Day, Natural Childbirth Week and so on. Which would link with your practice?
Strategy – Writing/Publicity	
Informational articles	Would your local village magazine or newspaper like an article that promotes wellbeing – and positions you as an expert in the community?
Newspaper columns	You could turn the above into a regular column – really establishing yourself as someone to turn to.
Charity events	Supporting good causes may be good for the soul – but it is also a PR opportunity. We know of practices that have nominated good causes or have sponsored charity events. One even sponsors children's education in Africa.
Be a source for local media	Each time there is a national story about an issue related to your therapy – workplace injuries, stress or ill-fitting shoes – you can generate a press release

	giving your professional opinion. Cultivating a relationship with the local media takes time, but ultimately they will be calling you!
Press releases	If you have a story, tell it! It could be an event, a milestone, an achievement or an interesting angle. Local media have a lot of airtime and column inches to fill, so craft a press release that makes it easy for them to create a story.
Be newsworthy	Even adverse events can produce a good outcome – one clinic we know got great coverage after they battled to reopen after a flood.
Commenting on social media	With the explosion of Facebook, Twitter and LinkedIn, you have many opportunities to comment on news stories, other people's postings or to participate in discussions. The more you comment (provided it is cogent and useful!), the more someone else will direct their network to it.
Strategy – Public Speaking	
Talking to interest groups (especially support groups for people with certain conditions)	Many practitioners use this to create awareness of their practice – target your audience, make your presentation very relevant, enjoy the experience and be sure to make clear how they can contact your practice!
Speaking at professional events	Building your reputation within your own profession can bring referrals – especially if you have a niche area of treatment.
Hosting meetings in a practice	Getting people into the practice to hear about a particular topic builds your profile and forms a relationship with potential patients. Get a speaker on a topic that interests your target market.
GPs CPD	Doctors are required to have a number of hours of training each year. Many get speakers in from drug companies. Why not present yourself and your therapy to raise their awareness of how you can help them and their patients?
Community groups	We know of practitioners who have got patients by doing careers talks at local Scout groups, or a general talk at the local Women's Institute.

Strategy – Networking/Getting Referrals	
Insurance companies/ Third Party referrals	Regular referrals from the major health insurers and other third parties like medico-legal case managers can supply a steady flow of patients – especially if you have a speciality like stroke rehabilitation, paediatrics or working with specific conditions.
Networking groups	Groups like Business Network International (BNI) bring people together to swap referrals. Other, less formal, networking groups exist too – networking is a massive growth industry.
Your professional association	Networking with your colleagues will increase awareness of you as a practitioner – and can lead to cross-referrals, especially when you establish yourself as an expert
Serve on committees	Whether that be a professional body or a local committee, giving your time in this environment allows you to develop links and identify new opportunities.
Referral partners	Bed shops, shoe shops, running shops, beauty practitioners and any number of companies and retailers could be the source of referrals (in both directions) and joint marketing efforts.
Social media	This is the new form of networking – Facebook, Twitter and LinkedIn (a business-based network like Facebook) are great ways to spread your net and link with more people. We see practitioners use Facebook very well to generate several new patients a week (with just a few minutes activity). We use LinkedIn and have found great returns by connecting with our target customers.
Referrals from patients	This cannot be underestimated as the engine that can power a successful practice. This is why the Patients Pillar is the centre of our Seven Pillars.
Strategy – Direct Contact	
Cold calling	The hardest part is picking up the phone. As a marketing tactic, it is rarely used by practitioners, and that is probably right, but we have heard of

	cases where it worked – cold calls to companies offering return-to-work programmes and workstation ergonomics assessments did generate enquiries.
Warm calling	This is calling someone you already know – so it's not totally cold! It needs to be done well, but can be an important part of following up. Remember, the call doesn't have to be about selling – you can just call and check up on someone's wellbeing. We often call or email former clients just to ask how they are doing. We don't expect it to translate to more work, but it sometimes does.
Lunch/coffee with potential patients /referrers	Don't let this become an excuse for a social! That said, targeted contact with key individuals is important in building a practice.
Leisure contacts (hobbies)	People you know through your hobbies will want their friend to be successful – so telling them about your work and what your perfect patient is like will help them help you grow your practice.
Canvassing (walk & talk)	A proven sales technique. Walk your neighbourhood and talk to people! Look for likely sources of patients (large employers, possible referral partners) then just go in and start talking. Connect with people around you. If they are small independent businesses like you, they are likely to welcome mutual support!
"Saw this and thought of you"	A clever Royal Mail ad and a great way of maintaining contacts. Cartoons, articles, latest research or just a friendly card – all good material to send on to a contact or a former patient to keep you at the front of their mind.
Announcement/ occasion cards	If something interesting happens in the practice (a new associate, expansion to an extra treatment room, starting Saturday or evening opening etc) a card to your former patients can be a good way to remind them you still exist. Avoid the rush before Christmas, and sensitivities over religious holidays, and send a New Year card – then you'll be the only one on the mantelpiece.
Newsletters	Regular written contact to keep people up to date with developments – and to entice them to return –

	almost always works. It could be a simple printed letter with your news, or a 4-page magazine-style mailing. Or, even better, an email newsletter that costs almost nothing to send multiple copies – and no envelope stuffing!
KitKat	We use this acronym to shorten the maxim Keeping In Touch Keeps Away Trouble. Trouble in this context is no flow of patients! Keeping in touch with former patients is one of the greatest missed opportunities we see amongst practitioners. How do you stay in contact once a treatment is complete?

We would hope, after giving you 50 tactics, that you are now not short of ideas of what you could do to generate enquiries for the practice. You are likely to be either: totally overwhelmed, thinking there is just so much to do; or buzzing with ideas and not knowing where to start. In both cases, we would advise taking a step back, thinking through the many options and then choosing a handful that you can really focus on, and that suit you and your practice.

Things to consider include:

- The time/cost trade-off we mentioned before.

- Your personal preferences – if you hate public speaking, or do not come across well when you try it, that probably won't be your best strategy.

- Look for a mix of activity across the various strategies – don't do everything in just one narrow area.

- What fits with the brand you are trying to create for your practice?

- What is most likely to reach your perfect patients? If they are young mothers, speaking at the local geriatric ward is unlikely to reach them.

- Measure what results you get from your actions and judge their effectiveness – and then react accordingly.

If we return to the Pipeline we drew out on page 42, we can now revise it and add the patient sources, strategies and tactics, before we get to the enquiry stage:

Patient Source
Walk-ins, Google, GP Referrals, Link with gym, Referrals

Strategies
Advertising, Public Speaking, Networking,
Direct Contact

Tactics
My website, Pay per Click Ads,
Search Engine Optimisation
Signage on street

GP CPD Event

Meet gym owner,
Treat gym staff

Ask Patients

Have referral cards

Enquiries
↓
New
Patient
Consultation
↓
Treated Patient
↓
Regular,
Returning
Patient

Hopefully, this illustrates how a marketing pipeline builds up into a plan of activities.

Exercise 13: My Strategies and Tactics to Generate Enquiries

Bringing together your own work on Patient Sources and the numbers you expect from them to meet your Objectives (Exercises 10 and 12), and the Perfect Patient you want to attract (Exercise 11), complete the table below to determine what strategies and tactics you will focus on in your own practice.

My Marketing Funnel needs to look like this:

Sources	Strategies	Tactics	Objectives
(Fill this in second) We suggest 5 or 6 sources.	*(Fill this in third)* Consider which broad strategies will suit those sources, and you.	*(Fill this in last)* Which tactics will attract your perfect patient, from the sources you have identified?	*(Fill this in first).* You may have more than one 'Enquiries Objective' (eg for you and your associates / different therapies separately).
1)			
2)			___ Enquiries/Week
3)			
4)			
5)			___ Enquiries/Week
6)			

Enter this information into your Plan (page 101).

A Brief Interlude on Sales and Ethics

We often find amongst practitioners a deep reaction to the concept of sales and marketing. It is considered unethical, pushy, unattractive, immoral, out of place in health care and generally uncomfortable. You may be feeling some or all of those reactions yourself, right now. We acknowledge that it could be happening, and then invite you to work through the next few paragraphs, and see how you feel afterwards.

We believe it is totally appropriate for health professionals to have reservations about how they market and sell their services. It protects patients and maintains the practitioner's professional standing. However, we also believe that most practitioners we work with, if not all, create a positive outcome in their community, because they improve wellbeing. Wouldn't it be immoral, unethical or uncomfortable not to do that as much as possible?

If part of your purpose was to improve wellbeing in your community (or something like that), then doing what you can to attract as many enquiries as possible is totally in line with your purpose. In fact, you would be undermining that purpose if you just sat in your therapy room and waited for the phone to ring. You would be doing potential patients a disservice by hiding away.

We do not advocate treating patients when they don't need it – that is what we would consider unethical. We do advocate seeking to extend the reach and impact of the skills and gifts you have in improving wellbeing. So we are totally comfortable in advocating that you sell and market your services. We hope you will be too. As it happens, you are likely to be doing this is in a society where such health care is not free at the point of delivery. As a result, you'll earn a living from it – what a happy consequence!

Materials for Promotion

We have now established WHAT you need to do in order to start generating or increasing the number of enquiries you see each week. Almost every practice ends up with printed marketing materials and/or a website as part of their strategies and tactics. We have seen this done badly so many times, we felt it was very important to include a simple step-by-step guide to avoiding the common pitfalls.

Step 1: Know the Purpose

Absolutely every marketing activity you undertake will need resourcing – be it your time, your money, your energy, or all three. It is essential, therefore, that those resources are part of your coherent plan to achieve your objectives – rather than an almost random meander through the various marketing ideas you know of. Your activity should be in the context of the Strategies and Tactics you have just formulated – so every piece of material you create should have a defined purpose within the overall plan.

Step 2: Consider the Audience

Marketing materials need to catch the attention and awaken the interest of the audience. Then they need to stimulate a desire for your service, and call the reader to action to make an enquiry. The look, feel and content will need to differ according to the audience you are targeting (and if you're not targeting, go back to page 29 and start again!). A leaflet aimed at elderly people with mobility problems should be very different to a postcard aimed at young gym members suffering sports injuries. And if you are tempted to create marketing material that will do both at once, go to the naughty corner and miss three turns.

Step 3: Consider the Channel

If you are creating a printed item that needs to capture someone's attention in a busy gym or a GP's reception, you will design it in one way. If you are creating something for the local bed shop to hand to customers when they ask for an orthopaedic mattress, it need not be so eye-catching, and can perhaps be more text-heavy. Where are you going to put your materials, and what job are you expecting them to do?

Step 4: Consider the Medium

We're not talking about clairvoyants here, we're referring to the format your promotional materials will take. If you are writing or designing for a website, you will use different layouts and different phrasing to make the most of the online environment, and to make your site Google-friendly. This won't be an issue if you are creating printed material like a newspaper ad or a sign outside the clinic.

Step 5: Be Consistent With Your Brand

Once you create a brand style and apply it across all your marketing, and your decor in the practice, powerful subliminal forces come to bear in your favour. Your patients' brains like to make connections, and hate disconnections – so you need to ensure the colour, typeface, design style and wording follow through from your advertising, promotional materials, practice documentation and appointment cards.

Step 6: Always be Professional

Get the best design and best quality you can afford. It is very, very rare for a good practitioner also to be highly skilled at designing, writing and printing promotional materials. Every piece of marketing material we have seen that was designed 'at home' has looked like it. It also devalues your efforts. We appreciate budgets are tight, and we know some design and print companies will charge the earth and give you dirt (so shop around), but always, always get the most professional help you can afford – it will pay off.

Step 7: Never Store it in Your Garage

Any marketing material will only earn its money when it is out there in the real world, where potential patients can see it. In our experience, once it gets stored in the garage, it is lost to the known world, only to be rediscovered in the great "Clear Out

Because We're Moving" purge, ten years in the future. Only produce what you need (with digital printing there is no need now for 4000-copy print runs) and get it out working for you as soon as possible.

If you are unsure of who could support you in developing materials for promotion, we have compiled a list of contacts who have worked for us, or for our clients, and who we trust (page 139).

Printed Materials – Some Basic Rules

There are probably hundreds of tips we have picked up from conference speakers, reading articles, our work with talented designers, or that we have seen in real case studies, but we have tried here to present the key ones:

- Target your audience – this bears repeating, so we make no apology for raising it again. You will get more response if you target a segment of the market by age, interest, condition or some other factor. We know that many therapies can treat from neonatal to ninety, and from head to toe. But there is evidence that if you claim this, the public do not believe you.

- Talk about benefits, not features. Unless you are marketing to someone who is a die-hard fan of your particular therapy, you are likely to have more success if you talk about symptom or condition relief, or other benefits. If someone has foot pain, do they care if you are a chiropractor, osteopath, physio or podiatrist? They probably just want the pain to go away, so sell them that!

- Unless you are a household brand, your logo is unlikely to clinch the sale. So having your logo as 25% of the front of a leaflet is about your ego, not successful marketing. Diminish the size of your ego and your logo in equal measure – save the valuable space for your marketing message.

- Less is really more – materials that try to cram in too much information, or are too text heavy, are routinely marked down in the market testing we undertake. Be concise, stick to key points and use the space to capture attention.

- Have a clear call to action or reason to respond – it may be a time-limited offer, or may just be a "call now to book your consultation". It is very admirable and ethical to just set out your stall and trust people will call. It is also largely ineffective. You need to ask!

- Be aware of any Advertising Standards Authority rulings on what your profession can or cannot claim. Practitioners in many professions are being closely monitored by sceptics – why give them the ammunition? If you are regulated, you are also required to stay within the rules. Find out what you can say, and stick to that.

- Market test your draft designs – we get several hundred untrained members of the public to critique practitioner's marketing materials each year. Almost without fail, they tend to spot the key positives and negatives of the designs. If they can, why didn't the practitioner and their designer? Sometimes we can get too close

– so getting an independent view (nb your Mum isn't independent) will help you gauge how people will react.

Websites and Online Marketing – Some Basic Rules

For some of us, the idea of printed materials for marketing seems very cutting edge and pushing the boundary. Alas, we have been overtaken and in the last 15 years the world has gone digital. The fastest growing demographic on Facebook is 50-60 year-old women, so even if you are targeting people other than the notoriously web-and-mobile-phone-savvy teenagers, you will need to think about your online presence. Here are our tips for that arena:

- Research has shown that when we view the internet, our eyes describe a so-called "Lazy F". We start at the top left and head along the top of the screen (because we read left to right). We then scroll back to the top left, head down before swinging across to the right about halfway down the screen. Before we get fully to the right, we come back and head down again, following the shape of the letter F. All your key content needs to be on that F.

- Internet attention spans are short and getting shorter. You need minimal written content, plenty of pictures/videos and short bullet points. People will NOT read long paragraphs or pages of text.

- Commercial web designers design around the "Most Wanted Response" – what do you want the visitor to do? The trick is to have all your content, on every page, leading to that MWR. For most practitioners, we would suggest the MWR is that you want the visitor to call the practice to make an appointment. So, have the biggest boldest text asking them to do that and include the telephone number.

- While we're talking about telephone numbers, unless you have online booking the number is the most important information on your website – because it is what you want people to use next. So have it, prominently, on EVERY page. Make sure too that visitors can click on your number to dial direct from their smart phones. If you make it hard to find and difficult to use, you may as well have a sign saying "Go Away, We're Not Interested".

- Increasingly, web visitors come and go without engaging with you. You will have invested resources in getting them to your page, so if your MWR of calling you doesn't work, have another means of capturing their info – offer something in exchange for their email address, which you can then use for an email newsletter.

- Your site absolutely MUST be optimised for the search engines (and Google is dominant). Either learn how to do this yourself, or use a professional. Work on getting your website on the top 10 listings for popular search terms in your area. Anywhere else will get a minute fraction of the traffic.

- You do need to come up on page one when people search for your practice name, but this is just the beginning. You need to be coming up under "condition, location" or "profession, location" searches too – that's how new people will find you. So, be optimised for "back pain Swindon" or "chiropractor Swindon" (if you are a chiropractor in Swindon...).

- Google Places/Google Maps is now the predominant route to search engine visibility – make sure you are listed.

- Social Media is catching up with search engines – you will increasingly need a presence on Facebook, Twitter and LinkedIn. By the time you read this, new sites may have risen to add to/replace even these.

- If you enter the world of Facebook, keep your private social networking separate from your professional presence. Do you want your potential patients to know what you did in Benidorm last summer?

We haven't given you any exercises yet on materials for promotion – because it should be fairly obvious. If you have yet to create any materials, consider your ideas against the tips we have given. If you already have some, critique them against the tips, and act accordingly.

Summary of Pillar 3: Pipeline (Part 2)

- Considering your patient pipeline will help you plan your marketing activity.

- By measuring the conversion ratio at various stages of your pipeline you can, hopefully, better manage patient retention.

- Growing a practice requires both generating more enquiries and improving conversion ratios.

- Strategies range from the more active to the more passive and there is often a trade-off between the investment of money and time.

- Which strategies suit you will depend on whether you are cash rich, time poor or vice versa. Usually a blend across the spectrum is the best plan.

- There are dozens and dozens of tactics you could use to market your practice. The key is to focus on a handful, and do them well.

- The patient sources, strategies and tactics create a funnel to fill your pipeline with enquiries.

- Promoting your practice allows you to improve the wellbeing of a wider number of people. We believe practitioners should be proud to sell their skills.

- Once you have your marketing activities planned, the quality of execution is key. There are many pitfalls to avoid, but some simple rules will help you get it right.

- Any marketing effort, whether in-person, online or in print, must be tailored to, and include a call to action for, the audience.

- Marketing materials work when they are out amongst your target population, not boxed up in your garage.

- Your target market can provide you feedback on draft marketing ideas – routinely test your designs with a handful of independent voices.

- Your website should be designed to attract traffic (be search engine optimised), engage the reader when they arrive, and then stimulate your Most Wanted Response (eg a call for an appointment).

Key Learning Outcomes from this Chapter:

I have realised:

-
-
-
-
-

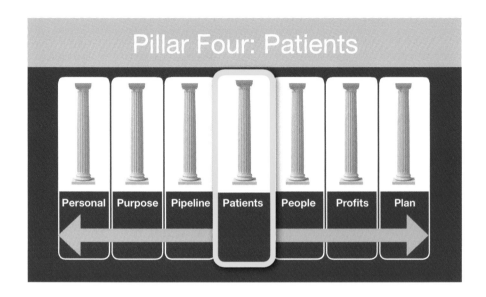

Patients

It is no accident that Patients are the central pillar in our series of seven, and we thank Rob Finch of the College of Chiropractors for expanding our draft 'six pillars' model. This pillar has two principal facets – the experience a patient has when they visit your practice (the non-clinical element of a treatment) and the efficacy of the actual treatment (the clinical outcome). If you are very good at one, and not very good at the other, the practice will not thrive. Excellence in both should be every practitioner's aspiration.

The experience patients have – clinically and non-clinically – is rooted in everything we have discussed so far. How you provide your service will be underpinned by your Values, providing the service should fulfil your Purpose, help you to achieve your Objectives and take you closer to your Vision. As patients have moved down your Pipeline they will have formed an expectation of the service they will receive, because of your brand, your USP and the promise you made in your various marketing activities. Now comes the moment when you have to deliver!

The Patient Journey

In the early 1980s Jan Carlzon transformed SAS, the Scandinavian airline, from one of the least punctual airlines in Europe to Airline of the Year for 1983. Carlzon developed the theory of the Customer Journey (see Reading List, Page 127). If we apply Carlzon's Customer Journey to the practitioner's world, we can come up with a "Patient Journey".

Exercise 14: The Patient Journey

Sketch out the steps involved in your patient's visit to your practice – from them being at home, through all the steps in the practice, back to being at home again.

The Patient Journey

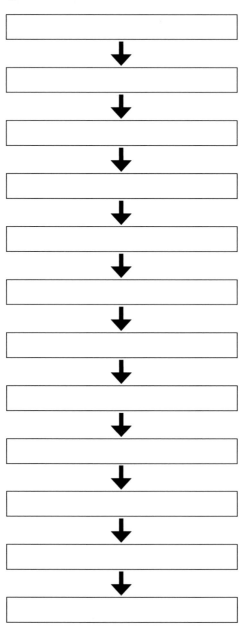

Now, compare your sketch with the one on page 75.

Hopefully you can see that a visit to the practitioner is not a straightforward experience! You will also see that the experience, from the patient's point of view, is so much more than the clinical treatment that you have been trained to provide. This is why one can see very professionally competent practitioners with stagnating clinics.

You will see that some stages in the journey are more important than others (the first welcome to the practice for example) and that in others seemingly minor details can have a disproportionate impact on patient perception (someone's tone when they first answer the phone – if they answer it all – for example). These key points were named Moments of Truth by Carlzon, because these are the moments when the true nature of your patient care becomes evident to the patient and prompts the patient to make a decision.

If you are able to 'wow' your patient, from the moment they first see your marketing through to the end of a treatment cycle, they are much more likely to become that engine of growth for your practice – the patient that always returns and regularly refers.

It is also important that we point out that each therapy has a slightly different version of the patient journey – the one we have included here reflects a practice-based manual therapy, but nutritionists, homeopaths, OTs, Speech and Language Practitioners and others will have very different journeys – you can determine what is right for you. For some practitioners, the emphasis will also be different – in some cases you have much less control over the physical environment (if you undertake home visits, for example). That does not mean you need not consider the environment however – asking patients or their guardians for certain changes to their home environment could hugely change the experience you provide.

Exercise 15: Standards and Wow Factors

Looking at the specific Patient Journey for your practice, what are the minimum standards you would want your patients to experience in your practice? If you really wanted to wow them, what more would you need to do? There is a Worksheet overleaf to help you. To start with, you might want to focus on the Moments of Truth first, and consider the others later. If you're not sure how to do it, here's an example:

Moment of Truth	Standard	Wow Factor
Waiting Room	To keep patients informed if we are running behind.	NEVER run late – or the fee is discounted.
	To have comfortable chairs, current magazines and toys for children.	To have coffee and buns, both fresh and unlimited.

Note: We are not suggesting you have to do both of these in YOUR practice, they are just illustrations.

Your Practice Standards and Wow Factors

Moment of Truth	Standard	Wow Factor

Do not underestimate how much detail you can go into on the Patient Journey – we regularly run workshops where practitioners spend three whole days covering the journey – and even then we only scratch the surface.

The diversity of experience a patient will encounter is as broad as the range of practitioners offering a service – and we have seen the truly excellent and the quite shameful. Here are a few pointers to get you thinking:

Before the patient makes contact:

- What look and feel does your marketing need to have to create a consistent brand?

- What promise does your marketing make?

- What expectations do you create in the minds of your patients?

When the patient first calls:

- What impression do you want to create when people call the practice?

- What will happen if there is no-one free to answer (Research says 66% of people will not leave a message on a machine)?

- If you have a message, what information should it convey?

- What should you/your receptionist say when answering?

- How can you ensure all the relevant details are gathered, and delivered?

- What is your intended outcome from that call (we suggest it is to get an appointment booked!)?

Arranging to see you:

- What standards do you want for the availability of appointments?

- How will you manage your working hours, and what will patients expect?

- How long is it OK for a patient to wait to see you – a day, a week, a month?

When the patient first arrives:

- What will they see as they approach the exterior of the building?

- What impression do you want your reception area to give?

- What should the receptionist say and do when a patient arrives?

- What information will you hand the patient, and what will be on display (eg what to expect, range of therapies available, scale of charges)?

- What will you do with patients who have difficulty reading (through poor eyesight, illiteracy or foreign language)?

In the waiting room:

- What do you want to provide in the changing room?
- How do you want your patient to feel while they are there?
- How can the furniture and decor contribute to that feeling?
- How will they keep entertained while they wait?
- What information will be available for them to read – whether as leaflets or posters?
- What sights, sounds and smells will you want them to experience?

In the treatment room:

- What quality of furnishings would you want in your treatment room?
- How do you maintain cleanliness and order in the room?
- What do you do to protect confidentiality of patient records?
- How do you put your patient at ease throughout?
- How do you discuss and obtain informed consent?
- How do you assess and improve your 'bedside manner'?

After treatment:

- What is the best way to close off a treatment?
- How do you get patients to "buy-in" to completing a course of treatments?
- How do you broach the issue of payment?
- How do you secure the next appointment?
- Would your patients appreciate the ability to pay by credit card? (They do, trust us.)
- How do you discuss ongoing or maintenance treatment?
- How do you stay in touch with patients?
- How do you inform former patients of changes at the practice, or developments in research affecting their condition?

General issues:

- What makes a patient feel valued?
- Can a patient be confident they get a consistent experience each time they visit?
- Is this consistency important to you?

- Is this consistency important to the patient?

- What training do you/your team need to make the most of the patient journey?

- How can you continuously improve the journey, especially the Moments of Truth?

- How will you know what the patient experiences – how often do you test it?

We fundamentally believe that getting the patient journey right, and continuously improving it, is the secret to a successful practice. It transforms the enquiries you receive into returning and referring patients – meaning you either don't have to work so hard to generate the enquiries, or the practice will grow and grow if you do.

It therefore makes sense that managing the patient journey becomes part of your overall Plan for the practice – and you can complete that element now on pages 116 and 117.

Patient Outcomes

We said at the outset of this chapter that there were two facets to the Patients Pillar. Whilst we cannot stress enough the value of improving the overall experience, it is of course fundamentally self-evident that the efficacy of treatment is critical to the success of your practice. You will need to be pushing yourself to be the best practitioner you can be, and seeking ongoing professional development at all times. But is that enough?

Almost every profession that we work with suffers from a lack of evidence according to the traditional, mainstream model of clinical research. We do not intend to argue for or against the Randomised Controlled Trial, traditional clinical research or the sceptic's arguments against alternative or complementary medicine. As non-practitioners with no particular axe to grind, we can see, however, how monitoring patient outcomes can start to deal with some of these challenges, and can benefit the practice and the patients.

In the absence of the level of funding available to pharmaceutical companies, full-scale clinical research seems a distant proposition for many therapy professions. However, the development of Standardised Data Collection tools and other initiatives, which we have witnessed in osteopathy in particular, will start to (and perhaps already does) build an evidence base of efficacy and safety. You can play your part by implementing data collection protocols within your own practice.

A positive benefit of investing your time and energy in such tools is that you start to collect data which allows closer management of the practice, and targeted marketing. In a busy clinic, perhaps data collection will highlight higher or lower success rates between practitioners – allowing you all to learn from best practice and drive up standards. Perhaps your data collection will show that 9 out of 10 patients with a particular condition self-reported an improvement of a certain amount in a certain period. Subject to the Advertising Standards rules regarding medical claims, you could then share that in your marketing and on your website. When a patient says "how many treatments will I need?" you can answer with greater confidence "well, every patient is different, but in this clinic patients with your condition typically receive 'this many' treatments and see 'that' improvement".

Exercise 16: Patient Outcomes

- What is the standard for measuring patient outcomes within your profession?

- How could you implement that standard in your practice?

- What system is available, or is required, for you to measure outcomes in a professional, standardised manner?

- Once you are measuring outcomes, what standards do you want to attain in the practice?

- How will you report your performance – within the practice and externally?

We recommend you answer the questions above in the following format, and then translate the results to your Plan on page 118.

Patient Outcomes

We will measure the following:

-
-
-

By following this procedure:

-
-
-

We will attain the following standards for these outcomes:

-
-
-

Software and Other Systems

Once one starts considering standardised data collection and measuring patient outcomes one can quickly start to see how the traditional paper records and metal filing cabinets become a barrier to efficient processing of data. It is possible that regulators will increasingly look for secure electronic data rather than paper records – to allow ease of data recovery, greater auditing and improved legibility. Even without those outside pressures, electronic storage of patient information facilitates and accelerates marketing of a practice – so it is something we advocate!

At the simplest level, electronic data management of patients can be a spreadsheet such as Excel, with data fields for all the relevant information – at least name, address, email and telephone number. One doesn't have to invest in an expensive, complicated practice management software package. But one might want to.

In our experience, practices that have good software systems find it easier to analyse patient data and monitor treatment levels – to manage their practice, in essence. Filing cabinets take up room, collect dust and present a huge task when you want to collate addresses for a mailing, or sort patients according to the date of their last visit. Software systems do this at the click or two of a mouse.

We have worked with three leading providers and their contact details can be found in the Useful Contacts section on page 139.

If one is flying a Boeing 747, or running a nuclear power station (few of our clients do either, we admit) it can be important to have Standard Operating Procedures that set out, in minute detail, what everyone should do, in what order, and what happens when something goes wrong. A therapy practice probably doesn't need the same level of complexity or detail, but we believe it can learn from the 747 example.

By having procedures, that the team are trained on and follow as a matter of course, one can ensure consistency in terms of the patient experience, ensure data is collected in a standard format and start to reduce some of the variability in the experience and outcome for patients. We don't suggest you standardise the treatment, or eliminate your personal touch (metaphorically or literally), but that you look to create written systems to support your service delivery.

At Painless Practice, we realised that our growth was going to mean our ability to provide consistency was going to be tested, so we looked for software and management systems that would allow us to manage a growing team of staff, none of whom work in the same building. Thanks to some excellent external support, particularly from Rebecca Russell (see Useful Contacts section on page 139), we were able to gear ourselves for expansion. We would like your practice to have the same capability. You can start simply, and build as you go.

James previously ran a business with about 500 active customers and over £9 million in turnover, and his team managed the business using less than 20 processes. Systems to deliver excellent service do not have to be complicated – arguably it is better if they are not. Even if you are working on your own, having a written process can help you ensure everything gets done correctly and helps you identify what resources you need to do the job.

Exercise 17: Practice Systems

What simple systems or procedures do you need in place to help you or your team provide a consistent service to patients? Use the Patient Journey as a guide, and sketch out the processes that need to be delivered routinely to ensure that consistency.

It could look like this:

Step in Journey	System Required	Documents Required
Telephone Answering ↓	Process for what to say, for checking messages and for diverting phone Virtual reception cover*	Message pad Phone instructions Instructions for virtual receptionists
Booking New Patient Consultation ↓	Process for offering info we want patient to have, and for gleaning info we need to have (name, contact details etc) Process for asking them to book	Crib sheet for giving info** Blank forms to fill in personal details/forms on screen in software Diary (paper or on PC) Suggested wording for asking for appointment

Use the table on page 72 to work out what processes would support you, and to start a couple of simple ones.

* Virtual receptionists are companies who answer the phone in your name and handle your calls as if they were your receptionists, but do it for dozens of clients (see Useful Contacts on page 139).

** The crib sheet could look like this:

Intention: To answer any questions and determine if our therapy is right for them, and if so secure an appointment.

Items to cover:
- Why have they called our practice?
- What are they looking for from us?
- How did they hear of the practice?
- What questions do they have? (See FAQs)
- How we work, what they should expect and our fees.
  (See FAQs)

Conditions treated: We work with a range of conditions, but generally treat issues arising from the musculo-skeletal framework, especially sports injuries.

Structure: Appointments are 30 minutes, new patient consults are 45 minutes.

Fees are £40 and £50 respectively.

They may be asked to undress to their underwear - they may wish to wear sports shorts/bra.

They may bring a friend if they are at all uneasy.

End with: Is there anything else you would like to know about our treatments?

If no - " Great, why don't we schedule you in - we have a space tomorrow at XX - how would that suit you?"

Actions: Enter details on database

Send new patient info by email

Schedule reminder text message

Afterwards, go to Your Plan and add details of the processes and systems that will help you manage the main elements of your practice (page 119).

Step in Journey	System Required	Documents Required
↓		
↓		
↓		
↓		
↓		
↓		
↓		
↓		

What would your processes look like?

Surveys, Mystery Shoppers and Audits

By now you will have set yourself standards for the experience you want patients to receive and the clinical outcomes you expect them to see (on average). You will have put some thought to the systems and processes that will support that. How will you know if it's working?

Three techniques have become common amongst big businesses that may provide lessons for smaller businesses like therapy practices. Customer surveys can help businesses listen to their customers, learn what they are doing well and hear about what they need to do to improve.

We have seen practices use patient surveys to get feedback from patients. They are best conducted on a regular basis, perhaps across just a sample of patients. In the modern era you can use online survey tools like Survey Monkey or Constant Contact (see Useful Contacts, page 139), or you can use the traditional methods of phone surveys or suggestion boxes in Reception. The more anonymous and more independent of you, the more honest your results will be.

Of course, one of the key things to do when you get the results is to act on them and improve things for patients – and then tell them. We know one practitioner who was told by her patients to sort two things – mend the squeaky treatment couch and get a credit card machine. She did both, and patients loved her. And the squeaky couch cost just a few pence – two squirts of WD40!

Another form of feedback – though not technically a survey – is to invite patients to provide feedback through online testimonial/user review sites like Qype or using social media such as Facebook, Twitter and LinkedIn.

The second 'big business' technique that has a place in small practices is the mystery shopper. You can arrange for someone unknown to book in as a new patient, receive a treatment and then provide direct feedback on the patient experience. Depending on how you set it up, the person can have been briefed beforehand on what to look out for, or can go in blind. One practitioner we know who did this actually had a friend do it – and ended up with enough suggested improvements to keep her busy for years. Another one used a company to do it, Painless Practice as it happens, and received a formal report detailing a large number of findings, with recommendations.

Finally, large businesses are good at auditing the impact of their work – having measurable outputs that they can track and manage. In the therapy context, this would be auditing patient outcomes. As we alluded to earlier, increasingly professional bodies are developing methodologies and tools to facilitate this, so you could explore what is available in your own field before developing anything yourself.

Director of First Impressions

Large companies, especially in America, have taken to calling their receptionists "Director of First Impressions". Whether it is true or not, it can teach us two important lessons. Your receptionist (which may be you) does create the first impression – initially on the telephone, and subsequently in person. If this is done badly, you will either lose the patient, or always be playing catch up. If it is done well, you have a great start on turning the visitor into a returning and referring patient.

The second lesson is that the job title "Director" implies a status for the receptionist above that usually afforded them. Often they are to be found at the bottom of an organisation chart, and are paid the least in a company. Yet a motivated, happy, well-presented receptionist, properly trained and managed, can be a priceless asset.

We will talk in the next Pillar (People) about how you train, manage and motivate staff, but an essential is to ensure that your receptionist wants the practice to grow, recognises their role (as important as yours) in making that happen, and has the resources to do so. Anything less, and you will be creating the wrong first impressions.

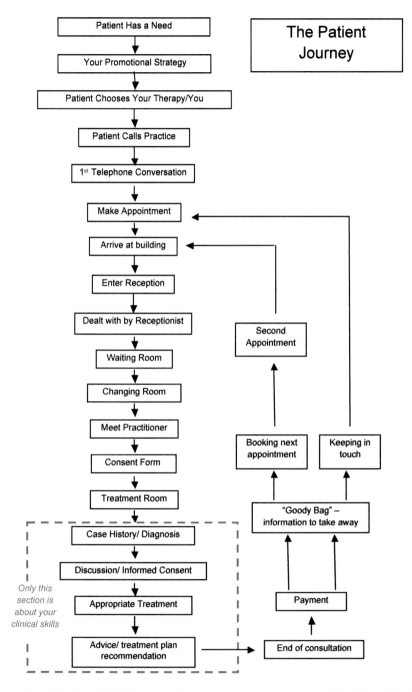

Note: The specific details of the journey will vary from therapy to therapy – you will be able to modify your own sketch to incorporate the relevant parts of this example.

Summary of Pillar 4: Patients

- The Patient Journey is the series of steps a patient takes when they visit your practice – typically 25-30 discrete steps – of which only a handful are related to your formal training.

- By mapping the Patient Journey for your practice, you can begin to manage – and improve – what happens at each step.

- Some of these steps are especially significant in shaping the patient's perception of their experience. These are called Moments of Truth and merit special attention.

- For any of the steps, you should be able to develop basic standards that you expect the practice to meet (consistent with your Brand, Purpose and Vision). If you are feeling adventurous, you can stretch yourself to provide a "Wow" factor, or two.

- There are a whole range of things to ask yourself or your team regarding what's important at each step (pages 65-67).

- Measuring and auditing patient outcomes will build a wider evidence base and can also be used for marketing messages (subject to regulations).

- To ensure consistency of service delivery, simple systems and processes can be used to support staff in getting things right first time, every time.

- As part of the overall management discipline in a practice, computerisation of patient information improves accuracy, aids manipulation and audit and facilitates marketing initiatives to individual patients.

- To really know whether your patients appreciate the experience you provide, or whether there are gaps you need to plug, patient surveys provide a useful feedback mechanism.

- For more detailed feedback of the overall experience, a mystery shopper can road test the systems you do have and set out your areas for improvement.

Key Learning Outcomes from this Chapter:

I have realised:

-
-
-
-
-

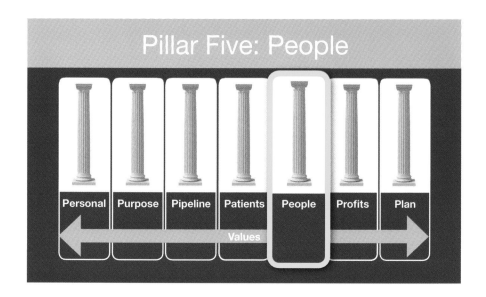

Pillar Five: People

Personal | Purpose | Pipeline | Patients | People | Profits | Plan

Values

People

If we lived in some strange science-fiction world, all the work you have done so far could be entered into a computer programme and then robotic staff and associates would turn up and follow the systems. Robotic patients would respond predictably to your marketing, call the practice, be treated and get better. Everything would run like clockwork, and the practice would print money at the end of the week for you to live on.

In the real world, that unpredictable, emotional and unreliable animal – the human – enters the picture, and the challenge of making it all happen gets that little bit harder. Let us not forget that arguably the most unpredictable, most emotional and most unreliable human is actually ourselves (you!), and even a sole practitioner clinic with no staff is not without its challenges!

So much of your plan is now complete (although we saved the all-important money piece until the end), but now we have to focus on how you really make it happen – in the real world. With real people who both exceed your expectations and underachieve – sometimes on the same day. This Pillar considers how you manage the people in the business, including you, to fulfil your Purpose and achieve your Vision.

Are you a Technician?

There is an excellent book that is a must-read for anyone running their own business (after you have finished this book, of course). The E-Myth Revisited by Michael Gerber is on the Reading List (page 127) and highly recommended. The E of the title stands for Entrepreneur, and the Myth is that people who start or run their own businesses are often referred to as entrepreneurs, yet very few of them actually are.

Gerber presents three levels of role within a business:

Technician: The person who does what the business does. This is a plumber who plumbs, a hairdresser who cuts hair, a practitioner who treats patients. Without these people, no service gets provided and the business seizes up fairly quickly.

Manager: The person who makes sure the technician has all he needs to do the job. This is the person who makes sure the plumber has a jobsheet for the day, the relevant tools and supplies, a working van and a system for invoicing clients and getting paid. Without these people the technician can only work for a while before he grinds to a halt.

Entrepreneur: The person who directs the business strategically, making sure the plumbing market is the place to be, studying trends in plumbing services, and perfecting the systems of the business so that it is successful. Without the entrepreneur at the helm, the managers and technicians can keep going for quite some time, but then find they are lead pipe specialists, and everyone is using this new-fangled copper.

Perhaps you can see where Gerber's myth arises – people think owners of small businesses are entrepreneurs, when in truth the vast majority are technicians. They run a business doing what they like doing, so they spend a lot of their week treating patients, a very small amount of time (often at night when the kids are asleep) being a manager and almost no time being an entrepreneur.

Exercise 18a: Entrepreneur, Manager or Technician?

Answer the questions below:

I spend my working week in the following proportions:

Entrepreneur	Thinking strategically about the future of the practice – developing new relationships, improving systems and planning.	%
Manager	Administrating the life of the practice – banking cash, paying bills, undertaking marketing, talking to staff and making sure there is work to do and that it gets done.	%
Technician	Treating Patients	%

Of course, you are more of an Entrepreneur than many, because you are reading this book about developing the practice – an explicitly entrepreneurial activity. But how did you score? Are you happy with the balance between the three roles?

Typically, we see the technician role filling the 35-40 hours of a normal working week and the manager role being squeezed into blank patient slots and late night sessions. The entrepreneurial stuff gets an infrequent airing at CPD events, perhaps the odd reading of a book, or a wistful daydream in the car or on the train. Does that describe you?

It wouldn't be surprising, for it is tempting to stick to the technician stuff. It is what you know (hopefully!), it is what you trained for (hopefully!) and it is what you enjoy doing (hopefully!). It is a safe place. So we spend most of our time there, sub-consciously. This only becomes a problem as you start to grow – and the technician time fills the week. Then you become a barrier to growth. You either work longer and longer hours, or your earnings reach a plateau.

Worse than that, a busy technician will neglect their manager duties – so eventually, when your current patients get better and the supply of new ones dries up because you were too busy to market, you enter the feast and famine cycle well known to small businesses and many practitioners.

There is a solution – to understand the three roles and plan to spend time in each space. If you were spending what you think is the right amount of time in each role, how would the table in Exercise 18 look?

Exercise 18b: How You Want it to Look

Entrepreneur	%
Manager	%
Technician	%

Through this chapter, we will explore more how you can get the right balance.

Roles

In recent years BT have run a TV commercial in the UK starring celebrity chef Gordon Ramsay, showing him doing all the back-office IT stuff in his kitchens. It plays to the stereotype that small business owners have to turn their hand to everything to get the business going. We will challenge that myth later, but for now let us just think of the roles that need performing in your practice, whoever does them.

Exercise 19: Roles in my Practice

Using this template, write out all the different roles that need to be done in the practice, as well as the key areas of responsibility those roles will have.

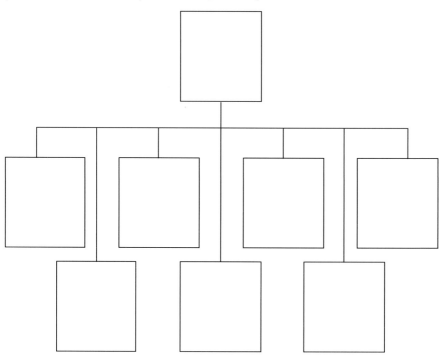

What roles would you put in each box? Do you need more?

What areas of responsibility will each of the roles cover?

Our stab at what they might be for a practice is on the following page (don't look now, do yours first!).

Those of you who run a practice on your own might now be getting an idea why you feel so busy! You can see that if you had to turn your hand to all the tasks above, you'd have to be very multi-talented, and have amazing amounts of time and energy. Which is why we want to break the "You have to do everything yourself to be successful" myth. In fact, the truly successful business or practice owners are the ones who recognise where their own skills lie and delegate the rest. That can even include delegating the boss role!

In reality, it is unlikely that you would be adequately skilled to do all of these tasks to the right level. This means that a key skill in building a successful and, dare we say, painless practice is building the right support team around you. They can be employees or freelancers who help when you need them. Your support team might consist of some of the following, and maybe some others:

Associate(s)

Receptionist(s)

Relief Receptionist(s)

Virtual Receptionist(s)

Practice Manager

Book Keeper

Accountant

HR Adviser

Solicitor

Graphic Designer

Web Designer

Copywriter

Health & Safety Adviser

IT Support

Printer

Bank Manager

Mentor/Supervisor

Business Coach

An example of the roles in a practice:

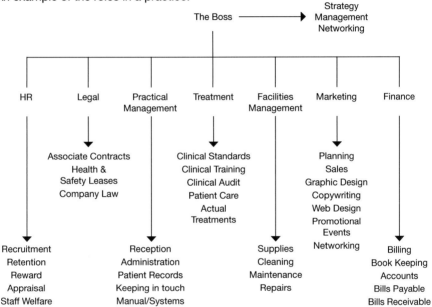

By looking at your strengths and interests you will be able to see which roles you can fill yourself (and still do the roles justice), which ones it would better for your existing staff to do and which you will need outside help on. For some issues it may be more economical to call on specialised advice from time to time rather than remain fully versed yourself (especially anything legal like HR, Health & Safety or company law). Many of the professionals listed above will have fees similar to professional practitioners (and some will be more, some less). Whatever the rate, if they save you time, allowing you to treat patients, they can pay for themselves.

In modern parlance, this is known as outsourcing, and is a very common model for small businesses, and many large ones. It allows you to have a virtual team far greater than if you employed people directly. It also allows you to get on with your core role of running the practice or treating patients.

In our experience (of our clients, and our own business), business owners hang on to tasks longer than they need to before outsourcing – because of their prudent nature or attachment to the role. We may not be able to change this in you, but we would reflect that letting go of these tasks is like putting a houseplant in a bigger pot – it creates the space for more growth. At Painless Practice, every time we have delegated or outsourced a role we have been able to concentrate more on growing the business and we have seen the benefits.

Exercise 20: People and Roles

Let us assume that you are not going to do everything on the roles diagram. If you are, please read through the last few pages again, and consider whether this is the most productive use of your talents! If you are going to spread the load, take some time to consider who is going to do what. As your plan is covering a five-year period, this may evolve, so the list may change over time (as your practice grows your cashflow should improve, and you may feel more able to outsource services or employ staff).

Use this table to set out who will be doing what. Translate this to your summary in the Plan on page 120.

Responsibility	Person	Responsibility	Person
The Boss Strategy Management Networking		**Legal** Associate Contracts Health & Safety Leases Company Law	
HR Recruitment Retention Reward Appraisal Staff Welfare		**Practice Management** Reception Administration Patient Records Keeping in touch Manual/Systems	
Treatment Clinical Standards Clinical Training Clinical Audit Patient Care Actual Treatments		**Finance** Billing Book Keeping Accounts Bills Payable Bills Receivable	
Marketing Planning Sales Graphic Design Copywriting Web Design Promotional Events Networking		**Facilities Management** Supplies Cleaning Maintenance Repairs	

Note: If you have yet to identify suppliers for any of the roles above, consider whether any or your patients provide the services, or get to local business networking groups, or use the Useful Contacts section on page 139.

Personal Management

The most important person in your practice, at least initially, is going to be you. It therefore seems appropriate to have a few paragraphs talking about how you manage yourself. There are a large number of books on personal effectiveness, so we won't take up too much space, but there are some key points that we have seen transform the lives of our clients, and their success in running a practice:

- Understand that there are different roles in the business, even if it is just you. Allocate time to the Entrepreneur, Manager and Technician roles, and the roles we have just described. Ensure they each get adequate attention.

- Clear clutter (mental and physical) – we are sure that you have heard the adage that a tidy desk represents a tidy mind. It also means less friction in running your clinic. Good filing preserves patient confidentiality, promotes an image of professionalism and reduces time spent trying to find things. Aim to handle paper once and don't let piles build up – whether letters to GPs, incoming mail, receipts etc for the bookkeeper, or old journals.

- Set aside time in your diary for practice management, and have an agenda of what you will do in your time. This relatively simple step has had one of the greatest impacts in several of our clients. If you want to focus on growing the practice, set aside an afternoon or a day to do it. Don't let trips to the gym, or a bit of shopping, eat into it.

- Have a Plan of what you will do, when you will do it and when you will review. We have this as a Pillar, as you know, and we cannot stress highly enough how this keeps practitioners focussed on the important stuff and much less reactive.

- Have some external accountability. Running your own business is totally different to being employed. You have no boss, and no one who will hold your feet to the fire if you slack off. This can allow drift to happen – we see it in almost every business we work with (whether practitioner or not). We have found in Painless Practice that having each other as business partners has helped enormously, because we nag each other, but even so we still need an external source of accountability too. We have business coaches, and we would of course think they are a good idea!

Delegating

If we are encouraging you to let go of some of the roles that need to be done, and to use other people, it feels like we should also raise the topic of effective delegation. Whether you are using associates, employing staff or engaging freelancers, they will all still need to be managed. Delegation is not abdication – it is still your business and YOU still have to take ultimate responsibility for what happens.

Delegation is a multi-stage process, and there are important things to remember at every stage:

Choose the right person If the wrong person is given the job at the start, you're stacking the odds against success from the beginning. This means you need to know the skills and attributes required to perform the task, and the skills and attributes of the person you are delegating to. Ensure they are aligned.

Set out the task Clearly articulate what it is that you want done – ideally in writing, and ideally with them confirming back to you their understanding of what you have set out.

Agree outcomes The end result is normally more important than the path there – so get agreement on what the outcome will be. This is especially important for outsourcing, but needs to be remembered for staff too. This is how you and they will know the work is done.

Agree resources For staff this may be an amount of money, training or equipment. For outsourced staff it will certainly include budget – so that you both know what the commitment is. One of the resources may be your time. The person performing the task may want input from you at key stages – agree this at the outset.

Agree boundaries There may be some things where you want them to seek approval, or to bring in other team members – agree these at the start. You may delegate the research for new computer equipment, but not want to empower them to place the order, for example.

Agree milestones You may not want to wait until the end of the project to review progress – so agree when you will meet to discuss developments. This could be based on time (review every two weeks) or on stages in the project (review when the initial website design is available).

Confirm understanding

Ask them to summarise all that you have agreed so far, and check there is no miscommunication or difference in interpretation.

Get out of the way

Now let them get on with it. Don't meddle and don't look over their shoulder, tutting occasionally. Get on with your own work, that's why you delegated this.

Be approachable

Whilst you shouldn't interfere, you should support them in performing the task, so be open to them coming and asking questions. But remember, the more you coach them into finding their own answers, the more you will be building their capability for next time.

Review outcomes and feedback

Once the project is complete, review the outcomes did you get what you expected/agreed? Discuss the process of getting there. Provide feedback so that they can learn what they did well, and what they can improve next time. Invite similar feedback on your role as delegator too!

Agree next steps

If the project or task is complete, move on. If there is a further stage, or the task will be repeated in the future, agree how that will work.

Managing Staff and Associates

We often talk with practice owners about their challenges in recruiting, retaining and rewarding "the right people". It is true that it can be hard to find people, at any level, that have the right attitude, aptitude and ability to do what we want them to.

Yet, it is often the case that part of the problem lies with the practice owner, not just the associate or staff member. We hear too many times that staff leave (voluntarily or forcibly) without any active management by the owner. If you do not want to manage people, or deal with performance issues, or support people through training and development, either practice as a sole practitioner with no team, or get someone in to do it for you. The fact you don't like doing it doesn't remove the need for it to be done. If you just abdicate the responsibility, you are opening the door for all manner of problems to walk in.

One of the challenges for many practice owners is the disjointed hours that most practitioners work – you may be in the practice every morning, and your associate is only there in the evening, for example. We would suggest that this doesn't mean that the two of you never talk – you have to structure regular opportunities to meet, review progress and discuss improving performance. Otherwise, problems arise.

Best practice is to have regular 1-2-1s between a manager and the team member at least every six months. Depending on the role or the situation, monthly may be more appropriate (for key staff such as receptionists, or if an associate has a performance issue, it is likely to be monthly). You can use the model for delegation, presented earlier, as a model for those 1-2-1 discussions. Make sure they are planned, and in the diary. It is easy for such discussion to drift, especially if they are likely to be uncomfortable for any of the parties – which means the poor performance goes on and on.

We think this is sufficiently important for it have its own section in your Plan – turn to page 121 and set out your schedule for 121s.

Another topic that occurs frequently is the issue of remuneration of associates. In most professions the associate acts as self-employed and is responsible for their own tax and National Insurance. They are freelance contractors to the practice owner. This is a tax-efficient way of working for both parties, but may not constitute the best model in terms of management and performance.

Most associates pay 'rent' to the practice owner, as a percentage of their treatment fee. The share a practice keeps ranges from 30-50%, in our experience. In theory, this motivates associates because the more they treat, the more they earn. But it doesn't seem to always have that impact. It can occasionally cause resentment from the associate ("why am I giving up 50% of 'my' income?" they think), often because the associate isn't fully aware of the cost burden of running a practice.

The model seems to create dissatisfaction for both practice owners and associates and usually ends up with the associate leaving to earn a higher percentage – sometimes just down the road with the patient list built up by the practice owner.

Most of the rest of the business world seems to make a living without adopting this model, so we urge you to consider other models as you build or grow your practice. Physios seem to employ people more than other therapies, but even they use the associate model a great deal. It is our belief that retention of good associates would be improved if salaried positions or shared-ownership models were more widely used. This is a topic that almost merits a book in itself, but if it is an issue for you, we regularly run workshops considering this.

Exit Strategy

Having mentioned ownership models, we will return to Covey's assertion that you should 'begin with the end in mind'. Within the context of your Personal Vision, you should consider what will happen in the long term, when your practice(s) are running painlessly and you decide it is time to do something else. That may be another business, it may be playing golf, it may be lying on a beach. Whatever it is, you will need to think how you will become removed from the day-to-day running of your practice(s).

For many, it just means selling up – perhaps a property, perhaps just the goodwill and fixtures and fittings of the practice. Will that be to just anyone, or to an associate who has come through the ranks? Will you retain ownership, but have the practice managed by someone else and just collect dividends periodically?

Will you want to keep treating until you drop, and therefore want to retain some sort of foothold in the profession?

Ultimately, the choice is yours. You can use your Personal Vision and the Plan to create the practice that allows you to do what you want – once you know what you do want.

Summary of Pillar 5: People

- A successful business requires adequate performance of three key roles:
    Technician (providing the service)
    Manager (providing the means for the Technician to work)
    Entrepreneur (providing the strategic direction for the business)

- Trained professionals, such as practitioners, typically like being a Technician, to the exclusion of other roles, and spend most of their time there. This will ultimately limit practice growth – the trick is to spend some time as a Manager and an Entrepreneur too.

- There are dozens of different roles and responsibilities required to build a successful practice – and rarely are they all best done by the practice owner.

- Some of these roles will be performed by you and others by staff, associates or support team members. This support team can grow as you and the practice grows.

- In our experience, delegating to the support team is usually done later than it could be – but when it is done it spurs further growth.

- You are likely to be the most important person in the practice for some time – so work on your own productivity through structure, self-improvement and accountability.

- Delegating is not abdicating, and you remain responsible for managing tasks to a successful outcome (but not by interfering!).

- Regular reviews with all of your team will allow you to improve performance. Schedule frequent 1-2-1s.

- Ownership and remuneration models within the therapy professions tend to be tax efficient but disappoint on many other levels. Consider whether the orthodoxy will actually work best for you.

- When considering how you will manage the people in the practice you should 'begin with the end in mind' – what ownership, pay and management structure best leads towards your exit strategy?

Key Learning Outcomes from this Chapter:

I have realised:

-
-
-
-
-

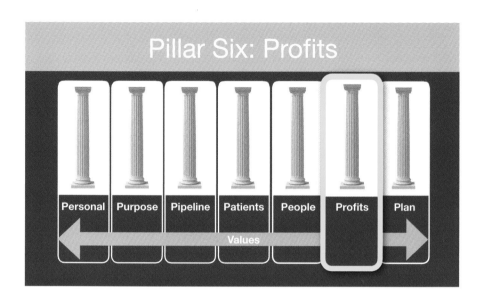

Profits

Back in the Introduction, we introduced each Pillar and gave a little description of what we meant by each one. Here is what we said about the Profit Pillar:

We know this is an unpopular word, but it begins with P and maintains our alliteration. We don't want it to be an unpopular word. Profit is what allows you to live, to feed your kids, to re-invest in the clinic and to have a sustainable presence in your community. So we think profit is a worthy aspiration, and the one important pillar that practitioners often avoid.

We have said before that our purpose at Painless Practice is to see every practice owner enjoying their work and achieving their vision. And in all the years we have been working to achieve that, the greatest block we encounter is the monetary side of practitioners' practices. This is why we made it one of the pillars, and why we hope you will embrace some of the ideas over the next few pages.

Before you think we want to turn every practitioner into clones of Gordon Gecko from Wall Street, avariciously pursuing money for money's sake, please consider the following quote from Jeffrey Hollender, which sums up our ethos:

Profits are the score, not the game.

We want you to enjoy the game of building a practice, to fulfil your Purpose and achieve your Vision. Furthermore, we think that money/profit should follow as a result. Profit is not the end, it is a side effect of the means. We have spoken to many practitioners who cling to the idea that ethically they shouldn't consider making money – so they don't, and they are unhappy. That is their choice, but it IS a choice. You can choose another path by reading and absorbing this chapter. Before we move on, we couldn't resist these two great money-related quotes from the legendary Spike Milligan:

Money can't buy you happiness but it does bring you a more pleasant form of misery.

All I ask is a chance to prove that money can't make me happy.

This may appear flippant – and this is not our intention. In our experience, money is the most common "hot button" for stimulating intense emotional reactions in people, especially when money is absent or threatened. And that is the reality of running your own practice. Success or failure is more readily measured in what you get to spend each month. People who have a salary rarely have that direct connection. You will when you run your own practice, and you need to think how you will handle that.

The best way to avoid this 'hot button' is to manage your relationship with money from the start. Embrace that earning a good living from your practice is just a sign that the score in the overall game is in your favour. Plan to achieve that score. Understand what score you need in order to survive (which we discussed in the Goals, Vision and Objectives sections).

One fundamental risk that practitioners tend to take, which exacerbates these issues around money, is to set too low a budget for setting up – being under-capitalised in business-speak. If you have emerged from a long period of training, you may have been working reduced hours, incurred tuition fees and run up some debts. This is a financially weak position from which to start a business – because then cash flow will always be critical.

Where possible, look to have a reserve of cash behind you – like starting a long journey with a full tank of petrol. That reserve may be actual savings, or a part-time income while you build the practice, or an understanding partner who can support the household while you grow. If you need the next patient to keep the roof over your head, or to put food on the table, it can be an unhealthy mental state to be in, so plan what you can to avoid it.

One of our own biggest lessons as we have grown our business is to distinguish between what we want and what we need. This applies to our personal spending (which then impacts on what we want to take out of the business) and our business spending. By managing costs and avoiding some of the sales messages we are bombarded with every day, we can reduce our cash demands, both in the short term and the long term. Does your practice really need the latest iPad to function, for example?

Exercise 21: How much do I want/need?

Re-visit the work you did way back in the Personal Pillar and look what you want to achieve in the short-to-medium term. What are the financial implications of those goals? Review your current and planned household expenditure to determine what you want/need (do both – need will be your baseline, want will be higher) on a monthly or annual basis.

	Need	Want
My expectations of what I can take from the practice		
Per month: £	£	
Per year: £	£	

Armed with this information, we can start to work out what the practice will need to do to sustain that lifestyle. We will now be starting to build a budget as a worked example, but we are starting with what is traditionally at the bottom of a budget – the profit.

To explain this with a worked example we are going to have to make an awful lot of assumptions, or it gets too complicated. Before using this method for any of your own planning, let us introduce a little caveat – none of the following constitutes legal, financial, accounting or taxation advice. Please check the assumptions apply to you.

In this example, we want to take home £3000 a month to sustain our lifestyle:

Profit after Tax £3,000

We then need to calculate what profit we need before the taxman takes his slice. In this example, the profit is paid as dividend from a limited company, so we shall assume a corporation tax level of 20%. In reality it probably wouldn't all be paid as dividend and wouldn't all be taxed at 20%, but we're trying to keep it simple – honest. (If none of that makes sense, please speak to an accountant).

Profit Before Tax (Tax at 20%) £3,750

Profit after Tax £3,000

We then need to consider the costs, on average, that the clinic bears each month. We will take some costs from our examples in the Back of The Envelope section (page 129):

Reception (virtual receptionist)	£ 500
Rent	£ 500
Business rates	£ 200
Professional fees/training	£ 130
Marketing	£ 250
Insurance (Malpractice, business etc)	£ 70
Equipment (bench etc)	£ 100
Utilities	£ 100
Clothing/laundry	£ 100
Sundries	£ 50
Total Costs	**£2,000**
Profit Before Tax (Tax at 20%)	£3,750
Profit after Tax	£3,000

You can see, we hope, that the practice therefore needs revenue of £5,750 a month if it is to pay you £3,000.

How might that revenue be made up?

Treatment Revenue (Treatment cost of £40)	£5,600
Profit from sale of items to patients	£ 150
Total Revenue	**£5,750**

So to summarise:

Revenue

Treatment Revenue (Treatment cost of £40)	£5,600
Profit from sale of items to patients	£ 150
Total Revenue	**£5,750**

Costs

Reception (virtual receptionist)	£ 500
Rent	£ 500
Business rates	£ 200
Professional fees/training	£ 130
Marketing	£ 250
Insurance (Malpractice, business etc)	£ 70
Equipment (bench etc)	£ 100
Utilities	£ 100
Clothing/laundry	£ 100
Sundries	£ 50
Total Costs	**£2,000**
Profit Before Tax	£3,750
Tax at 20%	£ 750
Profit after Tax	£3,000

Looks like we have a monthly budget! This practitioner now knows that they need to:

- deliver 140 treatments a month (because 140 x £40 = £5,600)
- sell enough products to generate £150 of profit (sales might need to be £300 to allow for the cost of the products to you)
- keep costs within budget

Straightforward, isn't it?

Exercise 22: Create Your Own Bottom-Up Budget

Now you have seen a worked example, you can use the Worksheet opposite to start to create your own. You should think through your own situation for any other costs you know of, in addition to our suggestions. Our Back of the Envelope (page 129) provides indicative (and that is all they are) costs – you may want to do some research to validate the figures for your own plans.

The issue of taxation, and therefore how you should arrange and plan your business affairs, is a complex and ever-changing scene. We recommend that before finalising your budget you talk it through with an accountant to determine the best approach in your personal circumstances.

From that budget you should now be able to calculate the number of treatments per month or week that are required to sustain the lifestyle you wish to enjoy. Do your original Objectives and the Pipeline in your Plan now need revision (see pages 111 and 115)?

How to Treat Your Pay

There are two important things to consider when running your own practice, with regards to how you treat your money. Firstly, we see far less problems with practitioners who see the practice's money as separate from their own. Whether a sole trader or a limited company, it is good discipline to keep the two separate, including separate bank accounts (if you are a limited company, that is required by law). You should then pay yourself money from those accounts for you to use domestically.

Secondly, we would advocate paying yourself for your treatments as if you were an associate (if you adopt the associate model) – work on the basis that 50% of your treatment revenue goes into running the practice, and the rest is yours to pay yourself (after tax). This may not be possible initially, because of your overheads (we will talk about break-even in a moment), but as soon as it is possible, we advise you do that. This means that when you have a growing practice, with several associates, you ensure everyone pays the same percentage contribution to overheads. (We meet many practitioners who end up paying themselves less than their associates, as a percentage of revenue, because they have failed to do this).

Budget Worksheet

Remember, if you are using associates, only include the revenue net of their percentage. _____

Treatment Revenue (Treatment cost of £_____)   _____

Revenue from Associates   _____

Other Revenue   _____

Total Revenue   (A)   _____

Rent   _____

Business Rates   _____

Administration (Office Admin/Receptionists)   _____

Bad Debts and Bank Charges   _____

Clothing/laundry   _____

Donations to Registered Charities   _____

Equipment (bench etc)   _____

Insurance – Professional Indemnity and Business   _____

Marketing (Advertising, promotional materials, websites etc)   _____

Networking   _____

Office Equipment   _____

Postage   _____

Professional Association Fees/Statutory Register Fees   _____

Professional Fees (Accountancy, Bookkeeping, Solicitor)   _____

Reference Books/Periodicals   _____

Staff Entertainment   _____

Stationery   _____

Sundries   _____

Training   _____

Travel   _____

Utilities – Water, Gas, Electric   _____

Telephone (Fixed, Mobiles and Broadband)   _____

Total Costs   (B)   _____

Profit Before Tax   (A-B) _____

Profit after Tax (Tax at 20%)   _____

Objectives (Part 2)

(To be completed after you have worked through the Profit Pillar)

Question	Your answer	Target Date
What percentage of new patients do you want to come from referrals?		
What percentage of patients in your database do you want to be actively receiving treatment (acute, chronic or maintenance)?		
What percentage of your room availability do you want to be utilised?		
What Patient Visit Average (PVA) do you want across the practice?		
What PVA do you want as a minimum for anyone working in the practice?		
What percentage of patients will you expect to return for their second appointment?		
What percentage of Did-Not-Shows (DNSs) will you accept?		
What other objectives do you have?		

Note: *You may wish to set a series of targets – building up to a five year plan. For example room occupancy may be 20% in Year 1, 40% in Year and 70% in Year 3.*

Now revisit the relevant part of your plan (see page 111).

Know Your Break-Even Points

Break-even is the point where your revenues just cover all your costs, before you make a profit. We would suggest that paying you your income is a cost for the business, so this should be included before you calculate your break even. If we go back to our worked example, the breakeven would be £5,750 per month. Knowing this means that one can be more pragmatic about the number of patients seen, reducing stress.

We work with a number of practitioners whose mood moves up and down according to whether the phone is perceived to be ringing enough. They get very stressed about everything being "deathly quiet", then we look at the actual numbers and realise they have done more than enough business to pass their break-even. So they needn't have fretted. If you can measure revenue fairly easily (either through your cashbooks, or through number of treatments given), you can soon see whether you are short of target, or doing better than hoped, and react accordingly.

We titled this small section "Know Your Break-Even Points", suggesting there may be more than one. The technical definition might not include your own pay, which would be one version. If we then add in your pay, we have two possible numbers to consider – the money you need, and the money you want. We suggest these two are the ones to use and monitor. And hopefully you will surpass the "want" break-even every month!

Budgeting and Forecasting

Having created the bottom-up budget for Exercise 22, which you may have done on a monthly or annual basis, it is not a huge step to extrapolate this into a financial plan for the year. You can spread the annual costs out over each month – or if you know they fall in specific months (such as annual registration fees, or quarterly rent or utility bills) you can put them in those.

This will allow you to forecast for the periods ahead – and then each month (provided you keep your books up to date, a discipline we would advocate) you can compare your actual performance against your forecast performance – and react accordingly.

Exercise 23: 12 Month Forecast

Use the Worksheet on page 99 to extrapolate your budget figures across the year. When you have finished playing with it, you can enter it into your Plan on page 122.

Your 12 month forecast, and your actual figures as a comparison, will start to give you information on your profits over the year. This will have a direct link to the tax you will pay, either as income tax or as corporation tax (talk to an accountant about the best arrangements for you). We strongly advocate setting aside the money for your tax bill as you go along, in a separate bank account, so that you build the reserve for when your payment is due. We have found this reduces an incredible amount of unnecessary stress!

12 month Forecast

	Jan	Feb	Mar	Apr	May	Jun	Jul	Aug	Sep	Oct	Nov	Dec	Total
Treatment Revenue (Treatment cost of £____)													
Revenue from Associates (Excluding % paid to Assoc.)													
Other Revenue													
Total Revenue (A)													
Rent													
Business rates													
Administration (Office Admin/Receptionists)													
Bad Debts and Bank Charges													
Clothing/laundry													
Donations to Registered Charities													
Equipment (bench etc)													
Insurance - Professional Indemnity and Business													
Marketing													
Networking													
Office Equipment													
Postage													
Professional Association Fees/Statutory Register Fees													
Professional Fees													
Reference Books/Periodicals													
Staff Entertainment													
Stationery													
Sundries													
Training													
Travel													
Utilities – Water, Gas, Electric and Telephone													
Total Costs (B)													
Profit Before Tax (A-B)													
Profit after Tax (Tax at 20%)													

Managing the Practice to Fulfil Your Plans

We think we have now covered as much of this side of the Profit Pillar as we can in a book of this nature – we've acknowledged that the word 'profit' might not be the most popular word but so far we hope we have proved it's importance. We have moved from working out what you want and need (which might be two different answers) to demonstrating how to construct a budget by using your desires as a starting point.

Once you know what turnover (sales) you want/need to generate, you can set the objectives that will take you there. There is a lot more we could cover, but without peppering the book with caveats and disclaimers, a lot of that is best left to individual discussions with your coach and/or accountant.

The other side of the Profit Pillar is to ask the question: how do you manage the practice to create the profit you aspire to, as painlessly as possible? For us, we think this comes from turning as many patients as you can into referring and returning patients. To illustrate this we are going to stretch the pipeline metaphor from earlier – and we are going to consider your practice as a bucket. Not flattering we know, but bear with us! Your marketing funnel will channel potential patients from your Patient Sources, through the Strategies and Tactics you have decided upon, until they enter your Pipeline. Having worked hard on your Patient Journey, you will have a high conversion ratio and most of the enquiries will spill out of the pipe into your Bucket – the swirling pool of day-to-day activity in the practice. Some patients will leak out – they will get better, move away etc. Profit comes from keeping patients happy in the 'bucket' for as long as possible. We are not suggesting that you continue treating patients who do not need treatment. But what we are suggesting is that in order for you to have a profitable practice, you need to create an environment and culture that encourages your patients to remain loyal to your practice and act as referring and returning patients.

We think this can be considered conceptually as a three stage process:

- getting patients to fully complete their course of treatment
- getting patients to return for maintenance and/or other episodes
- getting patients to be raving fans

Getting Patients to Fully Complete Their Course of Treatment

There is a significant benefit to both the patient and the practice if every patient fully completes their course of treatment, yet many practitioners see patients drift away after the new patient consultation, or after one or two treatments. Each therapy is different, but for many we work with, an average full course of treatments is 4-6 appointments. In purely financial terms, this can mean the practitioner is missing out on significant potential revenue from that one patient if they don't complete their treatment.

For the patient, the impact can actually be much worse than financial – because they will have aborted before their treatment is complete, risking incomplete recovery or a relapse. The figure below explains this graphically.

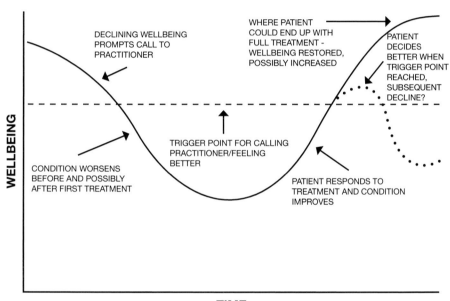

Patients start to feel a decline in wellbeing – whatever the symptoms are that your therapy relieves. Once wellbeing falls below a trigger point, they will take action to find a resolution (this, as you know, can often be well below optimum or normal wellbeing). There may be further decline until the new patient consultation, and even after first treatment as the body responds to your therapy. They then start to get better – perhaps after the first treatment, perhaps after the second.

If they complete their treatment fully (and we shall assume here that your therapy is effective!), their wellbeing will be restored, perhaps increased. If they fail to complete a full course however, they will miss out on the potential wellbeing improvements, and may even regress back to worse than when they first called you. At this point they tell all their friends they went to see the practitioner in the High Street and "it didn't work".

The key factor here seems to be who makes the decision to discharge the patient. If the patient fails to complete, effectively **they** have. Now, we believe, like many practitioners, in empowering people to take ownership of their lives and do not believe the practitioner should patronise the patient. Yet, you are the one who has the training and experience to make that judgement, not the patient. So, self-discharges by patients within a course of treatment show a lack of patient management by the practitioner.

The question is, how do you get patients to commit to completing a course of treatment? Some practitioners offer them discounts if they book a number of sessions in advance, but that is not something we would advocate. Rather, we encourage practitioners to find a form of words and a structure that allows them to stress the benefits of completing treatment, the importance of an appropriate evaluation before discharge and the missed opportunity for sustained improvement if treatment is not completed.

Exercise 24: Completing Treatments

- What proportion of your patients fail to return after the first or second treatment?

- What is your average number of treatments per patient, and does it differ from your colleagues?

Using a blank sheet of paper, work out a form of words that you can use to explain why patients should complete a treatment cycle, and consider where in the patient journey you will discuss it. Once you have the form of words polished, write them here:

Practice using these words (on people other than patients initially, if you feel awkward) and then implement it with patients for a month or two.

Observe whether the proportion of patients failing to return falls. Set yourself some targets to improve in your Plan (page 123). Please note, that 100% return rates are unlikely – there will always be a number of patients for whom a second appointment is not appropriate. They may just be visiting the area, or may need to be referred to another specialist, or may not be appropriate for your therapy. Set yourself stretching targets, but do not compromise the interests of the patient.

Getting Patients to Return for Maintenance and/or Other Episodes

During our work with practitioners of all persuasions, we often hear that the pervading ethos within their profession is to "find it, fix it, leave it", and successfully discharging patients from the practitioner's care is the goal for successful treatment. We happen to think that for many therapies, there is a bigger role for the practitioner to play.

Some professions (dentists are the classic example) have a very clear model based on maintenance or preventative care – it is widely accepted in society that a check up at the dentist every six months is totally normal. For many of the alternative or complementary therapies, we happen to think the same could be said. This is particularly true for the manipulative therapies such as osteopathy, chiropractic, physiotherapy or massage therapies. It is probably true for homeopathy or reflexology, but may be less so for nutritionists or occupational practitioners, which tend to be more episode-related.

It is our belief, and that of some in the professions, that a maintenance programme of some kind has benefit to the patient – the patient has an opportunity to manage risk factors before an acute episode develops, they have an opportunity to refresh their memory about exercises, stretches or lifestyle changes to manage their health, and in the case of some therapies they have an opportunity to spot other, potentially more serious, conditions early in their development.

For the practitioner, the benefit is that they develop a deeper relationship with that patient, increasing the chances of the patient remembering their practitioner when a need arises, or when they could refer a friend. This is another way of keeping patients within the metaphorical practice bucket.

To develop a maintenance or preventative culture within your practice you will need to educate yourself, everyone in the practice team, and your patients. You will need to articulate the benefits to the patient of a programme, and have a mechanism for deciding the best interval for treatments, based on clinical need.

Let us be clear: we are not advocating treating patients when they don't need it, just to meet your revenue target. We are advocating that you become an active partner with your patients in their well-being, and that you schedule reviews/maintenance visits/MOTs on a regular basis to build the relationship.

We have seen two measures which give an indication of the level to which your practice is operating on this sort of principle:

% of active patients –   this is the number of patients who have a future appointment booked, divided by the total size of your database/patient list (multiplied by 100 to get %).

Patient Visit Average –   this is widely used by chiropractors, and is a measure of how many times a patient visits, on average (as the name suggests!). It is calculated by taking the total number of treatments in a period and dividing by the number of new patients in the same period. You should end up with a number greater than 1! Note: This is not the same as the number of treatments per episode – because a returning patient after many years would increase the PVA, but might not change the average number of treatments per episode.

Exercise 25: Active Patients/PVA

• What percentage of your patient list are currently active?

• What percentage would you like it to be?

• What is the PVA for your clinic?

• Or each of your practitioners?

• How will you improve these figures?

Clearly, if patients are returning for maintenance treatments, or you are getting them to come back for subsequent episodes (which will increase your PVA), the diary will start to fill, the clinic will feel busier and you will be closer to achieving those financial plans you set out earlier in the chapter.

Yet that is not the most powerful consequence of improving these measures. By keeping patients actively booking appointments, and seeing them over more treatments over time, you will be developing a deeper rapport and better relationship with them – increasing the likelihood they will refer.

Enter some targets for your PVA into your Plan (page 123).

Getting Patients to be Raving Fans

As part of this process of developing rapport and building relationships, many clients find the following concept – The Raving Fan Ladder – a useful idea.

Potential patients initially have no idea of who you are, what you do or how well you do it, so they can be considered as Suspects – they are suspicious of you and your practice. Something will nudge them up to the next rung of the ladder – perhaps a newspaper column, a comment from a friend or seeing you do a talk: they are now a Prospect. They will call the clinic, ask the usual range of questions and hopefully your receptionist will nudge them up to the next rung on the ladder – they are a Customer/patient.

As we have been discussing, they may not fully engage with the practice, your therapy or you as a person and the relationship could end. What you are looking to do is nudge them to the next rung on the ladder – where they are a Member of your practice – engaged on an ongoing basis, with some level of connection and allegiance to the clinic.

Further nudges can turn them into being an Advocate – where they respond to enquiries from friends by suggesting you, but perhaps don't actively promote you. They are reactively promoting you, but not yet proactively. If you can nudge them to the top level, they will proactively proclaim your skills from the rooftops and will have become a Raving Fan. Your dream might be to have a few well-connected Raving Fans who profess your virtues to a wide network, consistently generating referrals.

- How many of your patients are on the higher rungs of this ladder?

- What could you be doing to nudge people up the ladder?

- How does your plan for the Patient Journey (page 64) help nudge people up the ladder?

Practitioners who can develop a number of Raving Fans for their practice will find they have more sustained, profitable practices. They will not need to spend so much to gain new patients, improving what they can earn and reducing the effort required on wider marketing. Raving Fans take focus and effort to create and sustain, but maintaining them is more painless than chasing new patients through other means.

Exercise 26: Raving Fan Game

One of the Painless team, Vicky, has developed a chart to help people manage how they nudge key people up the ladder (see next page). The idea is to identify 10 or so people from your network who could be Raving Fans (some may still be Suspects) and tick the box that applies to them. You then need to review the chart each week and set yourself targets for moving people across the sheet until they are Raving Fans. Once you complete this sheet, you can draw up a new list to work on!

Some Other Assorted Items Relating to Profit

Before we finish with the Profit Pillar, we would like to discuss a final few issues that may help you run the practice more successfully.

Firstly, we have already mentioned how many practitioners charge too little for their services, diminishing the respect they may attract in the professional marketplace and reducing their ability to earn a living wage. We therefore urge all practitioners to very carefully consider what price point they should be aiming at for their clinic. Once set, it is then imperative that this is reviewed at least annually to ensure any increase in costs is reflected in their rates, and that their earning power increase over time. In our experience, annual increases of one pound or so are far easier to introduce than an irregular jump of five pounds. Are you happy with your pricing?

Secondly, many practitioners rent rooms to other practitioners on an hourly or per-session basis. When we invite clients in such situations to calculate the actual cost of opening the clinic (including all property costs, receptionist etc) they often find they are charging less in rent than it costs to open the clinic. This effectively means they are subsidising the other practitioners. Is this fair or wise? If you do rent rooms, please calculate the total cost of running the building, and divide by the number of hours you are open – this will give an idea of what you should be charging for rent.

Thirdly, there are two statistics that can be useful for practitioners to monitor in their practice:

- % occupancy gives you an idea of how busy you actually are in the clinic. Someone doing 20 treatments could be full if that is all they have available, or very quiet if they have four treatment rooms available 40 hours a week. Once clinics get above 85% occupancy they tend to have issues with availability of slots for new patients, but many operate at far below this figure. This is failing to make the most of the space in the clinic.

- Average revenue per patient (ARPP) tells you what the average spend per patient is in the clinic – say 4 treatments at £40, so £160. If they also buy some products from you, that revenue would be added. Knowing this figure allows you to compare the average revenue with the return on your marketing. If sponsoring a local football team costs £600 a year and only generates 1 patient at an ARPP of £160, is it worth continuing?

Raving Fan Game

Contact	Organisation	Suspect (tick)	Prospect (tick)	Customer (tick)	Member (tick)	Advocate (tick)	Raving Fan (tick)	Date of last Contact
1								
2								
3								
4								
5								
6								
7								
8								
9								
10								
11								
12								
13								
14								
15								

Summary of Pillar 6: Profit

- Be open to making money in your practice.

- Understand what you want/need from the practice in order to achieve your Vision. Aim for this as a minimum.

- If you start with what you want from the practice financially (your profit) and work up from there, you can determine what level of revenue you want (and thus what marketing may be required).

- Consult an accountant before progressing too far with your plans to ensure you are operating as tax efficiently as possible.

- Keep your personal money and your practice money separate, even if you are a sole trader. It helps reduce confusion and nasty surprises, and is a legal requirement if you are a limited company.

- Develop a forecast of your budget for the next 12 months (at least) and then monitor your actual performance against that budget.

- Keeping patients active within the practice 'bucket' ensures that they benefit fully from treatment, and that your practice grows.

- Patients should only be discharging themselves in consultation with you, their practitioner. They deserve to receive the right amount of treatment.

- Where possible and appropriate, getting patients to return for maintenance or other episodes will strengthen the relationship and rapport with patients and drive practice growth.

- Helping patients move up the Raving Fan Ladder (by being proactive) will reap rewards in word-of-mouth referrals.

- Regularly review all prices.

- There are some key numbers to know for your clinic: revenue, costs, profit, % of active patients, Patient Visit Average, % occupancy and Average Revenue Per Patient.

Key Learning Outcomes from this Chapter:

I have realised:

-

-

-

-

-

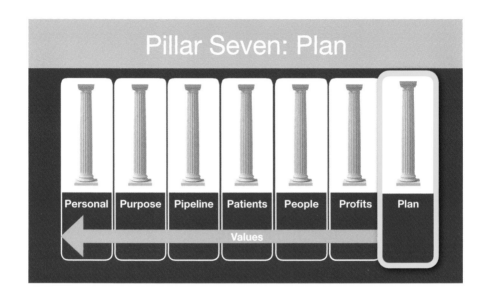

Plan

This should be the most exciting Pillar in the whole book, and we shouldn't be writing much of the content, you should. Hopefully you will be able to complete each section here as you work through the other Pillars, until you have a plan that you can use to manage the success of your practice. If you would like these sheets as an electronic file for you to edit, please visit www.painlesspractice.com/resources/exercises

We cannot stress enough how the use of a properly written and regularly reviewed plan is a key factor in sustained success. Articulating your thoughts and dreams from your practice into a document, and committing it to paper just seems to create a different dynamic for practice owners. Having regular opportunities to review progress, and monitor the overall direction of the plan is then another significant step. Whether with shareholders, a spouse, the practice team or a business coach, checking performance and determining corrective action leads to sustained success. We have seen this time and again with clients. We hope that is the case for you too. Now, over to you...

Your Personal Vision:

By ....<insert date>, I want the following things to be true of my life outside of my practice:

-   •
-   •
-   •
-   •
-   •
-   •

In order to achieve those things in the rest of my life, I want the practice to meet these criteria:

-   •
-   •
-   •
-   •
-   •
-   •

Whilst I build this, I shall remember that my personal values are:

-   •
-   •
-   •

(Note: When you share your plan with others, you may want to detach this page and keep it private)

Practice Purpose and Vision

The purpose of .... <insert practice name>

is...

....

....

....

Practice Objectives (not tasks or actions)

Year	Objectives
Year 1 (20.........)	
Year 2 (20.........)	
Year 3 (20.........)	
Year 4 (20.........)	
Year 5 (20.........)	

Market Analysis

Description of the local marketplace:

....
....
....
....
....
....
....
....
....
....

Key features of our location(s) will be:

....
....
....
....
....
....
....
....
....
....

Our Unique Selling Proposition

Patients will come to .... because

....

....

....

....

....

....

....

....

....

....

....

The words to sum up our clinic brand are:

....

....

....

....

....

....

....

....

....

....

....

....

The key sources of patients will be:

- Word of Mouth
- Returning Patients
- Friends/Family
- Leisure Contacts
-

-
-
-
-
-

Qualities of my perfect patients are:

-
-
-
-
-

-
-
-
-
-

To attract those perfect patients I will need to:

-
-
-
-
-

-
-
-
-
-

My key sources of patients will be:

Source 1	%
Source 2	%
Source 3	%
Source 4	%
Source 5	%
Source 6	%
Total	

Sources	Strategies	Tactics	Objectives
1) 2) 3)			___ Enquiries/Week
4) 5) 6)			___ Enquiries/Week

Our Patient Journey includes the following steps:

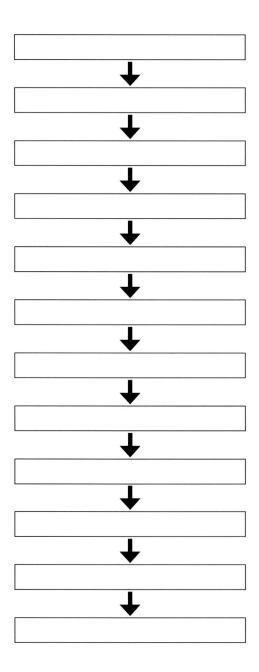

To manage and improve the Patient Journey, we have identified the following Moments of Truth, and the standards we will uphold:

Moment of Truth	Standard	Wow Factor

Patient Outcomes

We will measure the following:

-
-
-
-
-

By following this procedure:

-
-
-
-
-

We will attain the following standards for these outcomes:

-
-
-
-
-

Practice Systems

We will use the following systems for managing our diary, our patient information and our clinical outcomes:

Diary	Patient Information	Clinical Outcomes

We will also use the following for other elements of our practice:

Area of Work:			
System:			

We will produce a Practice Manual, with all our processes included, by ....
<insert date>

People and Roles

Overall Management and leadership will be provided by:

....<name>

Service delivery (treatment) will be provided by:

....<name>

....<name>

....<name>

....<name>

....<name>

....<name>

Staff will be employed for the following roles:...

Role .... <role>... <name>

Role .... <role>... <name>

Role .... <role>... <name>

Role .... <role>... <name>

Role .... <role>... <name>

In addition to service delivery, the following support services are currently retained:

Role .... <role>... <name>

Role .... <role>... <name>

Role .... <role>... <name>

Role .... <role>... <name>

Role .... <role> .... <name>

Role .... <role>... <name>

Role .... <role>... <name>

Role .... <role>... <name>

Role .... <role>... <name>

Role .... <role>... <name>

Managing Performance

Regular Reviews (1-2-1s) will be held as follows:

Team member *(these could be staff, associates or others)*	Last 1-2-1 Date	Next 1-2-1 Date	Subsequent 1-2-1 Date
.... \<name\>			
.... \<name\>			
.... \<name\>			
.... \<name\>			
.... \<name\>			
.... \<name\>			
.... \<name\>			
.... \<name\>			
.... \<name\>			
.... \<name\>			
.... \<name\>			

12 month Forecast

	Jan	Feb	Mar	Apr	May	Jun	Jul	Aug	Sep	Oct	Nov	Dec	Total
Treatment Revenue (Treatment cost of £____)													
Revenue from Associates (Excluding % paid to Assoc.)													
Other Revenue													
Total Revenue (A)													
Rent													
Business rates													
Administration (Office Admin/Receptionists)													
Bad Debts and Bank Charges													
Clothing/laundry													
Donations to Registered Charities													
Equipment (bench etc)													
Insurance - Professional Indemnity and Business													
Marketing													
Networking													
Office Equipment													
Postage													
Professional Association Fees/Statutory Register Fees													
Professional Fees													
Reference Books/Periodicals													
Staff Entertainment													
Stationery													
Sundries													
Training													
Travel													
Utilities – Water, Gas, Electric and Telephone													
Total Costs (B)													
Profit Before Tax (A-B)													
Profit after Tax (Tax at 20%)													

Completing Treatments and increasing patient visit average

We will set the following targets for helping patients engage in treatments:

Team Member	% returning for 2nd Treatment	By: (Date)
Practice Overall:		
Principal: .... (name)		
Associate: .... (name)		
Associate: .... (name)		
Associate: .... (name)		
Associate: .... (name)		

We will then have the following target for the overall patient visit average:

Team Member	Patient Visit Average	By: (Date)
Practice Overall:		
Principal: .... (name)		
Associate: .... (name)		
Associate: .... (name)		
Associate: .... (name)		
Associate: .... (name)		

This plan will be reviewed on the following dates:

Review 1 ....

Review 2 ....

Review 3 ....

Review 4 ....

The plan will be re-written for the next period on the following date: ....

Summary

You should now have the pillars in place for your practice to grow – you know where you want to go, who you want as patients, how you will market to them and the experience they will receive when they come for treatment.

If you have started taking action with marketing your practice, or improving the patient experience, you may even be seeing parts of your Vision coming to fruition. Now it is a question of applying consistent attention, action and patience.

Before we finish, perhaps we can reiterate the Seven Pillars and the importance of each of them:

Pillar 1	Personal	You will only enjoy the work of growing your practice if it is aligned with what drives and motivates you personally. If you don't enjoy the work, you will be forever pushing a rock up a hill trying to achieve success. Make sure your practice contributes to what you want in life on a personal level.
Pillar 2	Purpose	We work with successful businesses all the time, and a common factor in their success is an understanding of what success is and why they are doing it. The business owners have a clear sense of purpose, and they are able to convey that to those around them.
Pillar 3	Pipeline	So much of the work we do with practitioners is on finding new patients. Having a clear structure and plan of how you will attract interest in your clinic, and how you will manage any enquiries into becoming regular patients is critical to success for any practice, large or small.
Pillar 4	Patients	Fostering wellbeing is central to the work of all practitioners – so positive patient outcomes are essential in your practice. But the patient experience is so much wider than just the clinical outcome. Make sure your whole team are on top of their game in looking after all aspects of the patient journey.
Pillar 5	People	Managing those who will contribute to your success, whether associates, receptionists, website designers or yourself, will be a key part of your challenge ahead. Many practitioners shy away from this area of responsibility (not quite as many as shy away from the Profit side, but almost!). There is very little else in a therapy practice, other than people, so focus on managing your people as well as you can.
Pillar 6	Profits	If you are able to earn an income, reinvest in developing the practice and protect yourself from the ups and downs of a small business, you will be in the best place to serve your

community and keep getting people better. Your ability to do this comes from making a profit – so managing the practice for success in this pillar sets you up to achieve all your other aspirations.

Pillar 7   Plan   You should now have one. At the very least you have the opportunity to create one. That puts you one step ahead of so many other practitioners and small business owners. The key thing now is to follow the plan! Take some action – then review progress.

We know that some bits of this book will appeal more to you than others, but please don't skimp on any of the pillars – you just make the whole structure uneven, unstable and less likely to achieve success.

There is so much we could have crammed into this book, but chose to leave out to make it readable. We believe the material we have included will give you a great start. If you want access to more, please subscribe to our email newsletter, join our LinkedIn Group, attend a workshop or give us a call about working together.

We mentioned in the Purpose Pillar that Painless Practice's purpose is to see every practice owner enjoying their work and achieving their vision. We do believe that the steps outlined under our Seven Pillars in this book will give you the opportunity to enjoy your work and achieve your vision. But we cannot make it happen for you. We implore you to take action having read this far, and grow the practice you want, improve the health and wellbeing of your community and realise the potential that is within you.

We'll leave you with a quote from Mark Twain:

"Twenty years from now you will be more disappointed by the things that you didn't do than by the ones you did do."

What are you going to do?

Reading List

Links to an Amazon book list of all the publicly available books below can be found at www.painlesspractice.com/resources/reading-list

Practice development texts:

Get Clients Now!
CJ Hayden, Amacom, ISBN 9780814473740

Getting Business to Come to You
Paul & Sarah Edwards & Laura Clampitt Douglas, Jeremy P Tarcher,
ISBN 978087477845X

Attracting Perfect Customers
Stacey Hall and Jan Brogniez, Berrett-Koehler, ISBN 9781576751244

Business Development Handbook: Creating Osteopathic Value
James Butler and Michael Watson, British Osteopathic Association, (BOA)

Running a Successful Homeopathic Practice
James Butler and Sarah Whittaker, The Society of Homeopaths, (SOH)

Business Books:

The E-Myth Revisited: Why Most Small Businesses Don't Work and What To Do About It
Michael E Gerber, Harper Collins, ISBN 9780887307287

Moments of Truth
Jan Carlzon, Harper Collins, ISBN 9780060915803

Starting a Business for Dummies
Colin Barrow, John Wiley & Sons, ISBN 9780470978108

Growing Your Business
Gerard Burke, Liz Clarke, Paul Barrow and David Molian, Routledge,
ISBN 9780415405181

General texts:

The Seven Habits of Highly Effective People
Stephen R Covey, Simon & Schuster Ltd, ISBN 9780684858395

Articles:

Maintenance Treatment – Good or Bad?
Christopher D Dyer DO, Osteopathy Today, October 2007, p20

A wide range of further articles and newsletters are freely available via the Painless Practice website (www.painlesspractice.com).

For ongoing top tips and discussions, please join the Painless Practice Group on LinkedIn – go to www.linkedin.com and search for Painless Practice under Groups.

Back of The Envelope

In order to help you decide what might be the most appropriate Vision for you, this section provides some approximate revenues and costs for the various scenarios that may be open to a practitioner. These are only an indication and any detailed planning for your own purposes should be based on costs specific to your own situation. Many factors will affect the exact costing in your location and you are advised to research and prepare a more detailed and accurate business plan reflecting your personal circumstances.

The figures presented below represent the higher end of what a practitioner might achieve, in terms of revenue and patients, in order to demonstrate what may be possible if you achieve your vision. For some these levels will be some time off, and may never be what they strive for. You can manage the figures accordingly.

For the purposes of these calculations, the following assumptions have been made:

Revenue

- A 'working day' for a practitioner is 8 hours, with a 30 minute appointment time – meaning 16 treatments a day.

- This is unlikely to be achieved, so a 75% occupancy, or 12 treatments a day is more likely.

- An indicative charge of £30 for a 30 minute treatment has been used.

- This means revenue of £360 per day.

- If a practitioner works for 46 weeks a year (assuming no income when sick or on vacation), then the annual revenue for one day a week is 46 x £360, which is £16,560.

- For the purposes of this exercise, the annual revenue for one day a week is £16,000.

- This would imply an annual revenue of £80,000 if working five days a week. However, it is more realistic to allow for four days a week, implying an annual revenue of £64,000.

- For ease of calculation it is assumed associates pay 50% of revenue in 'rent' to the principal.

Premises Costs

- Costs have been calculated per treatment space (a treatment couch in a room). It is accepted that two or more practitioners may work part time and share a space.

- A single-treatment-space practice would consist of the following:
    - Treatment room, 5m x 4m (20m²)
    - Waiting room, 3.2m x 3.2m (10m²)
    - Toilet, 1m x 2m (2m²)
    - Hall, 1m x 2m (2m²)
    - Making a total of 20 m² treatment space and 14 m² other space
- For each further treatment space an approximate calculation of 1 further treatment room and 50% of other space has been made:
    - 1 treatment space   = (1 x 20) + (1 x 14)   = 34 m²
    - 2 treatment spaces   = (2 x 20) + (1.5 x 14)   = 61 m²
    - An annual rental cost of £150/ m² has been assumed.
- A business rates cost of £60/ m² has been assumed. (Some rents will include business rates, so explore this for your particular situation).
- To own the property, rather than renting, you can convert a space in your own home, add an extension, convert a whole property or buy a building currently being used as a clinic:
    - Assumed cost of converting existing space: £10,000 over 7 years
    - Assumed cost of adding an extension: £20-100,000 over 20 years
    - Assumed cost of purchasing property: £250-400,000 over 25 years
    - Approx loan cost of converting existing space: £2,100/year
    - Approx loan cost of adding an extension: £1,800 – £8,500/year
    - Approx loan cost of purchasing property: £19,000 – £30,400/year

Receptionist/ Telephone Answering

Receptionist costs have been calculated as approximately £16,500 on the basis of a 40 hour week at a wage of £7 per hour.

7 x 40 x 52 = £14,560 (plus employer NI costs of approx 13% – £1,900)

If you have one receptionist, you will need to budget for sickness/holiday cover at about £2,500 – for perhaps 8 weeks a year (6 wks leave, 2 weeks sickness).

7 x 40 x 8 = £2,240 (plus employer NI costs of 13% – £291)

Sole practitioners may choose not to have a receptionist, but to use a telephone answering service to field calls and take appointments. This is usually charged on a per-call basis.

Based on 12 appointments a day, you might expect 15 calls for each day, a total of 300 calls a month. The leading virtual receptionist for practitioners has a package for up to 500 calls for £525 per month + VAT, plus some other additional costs depending on the service. We have assumed a monthly fee, including VAT, of £1,000, therefore an annual cost of £12,000.

Other Budget Items

The following approximate annual costs have been assumed for other items (some of these may be an overestimate and are provided for illustration only):

- Printing promotional materials   £2,000
- Professional fees/ training   £1,500
- Advertising   £1,000
- Malpractice Insurance   £ 500
- Other Insurance   £ 500
- Equipment (bench etc)   £1,000
- Utilities   £1,000
- Sundries   £1,000
- Clothing/laundry   £ 500

Of course we also think that business coaching is an important part of growing a successful practice, but have not been presumptuous enough to include it in these bugets. We would advise setting aside £1000 a year for this purpose.

Example Budgets

Associate in Single/Multiple Practice

Revenue

Working 4 days a week	£64,000

Expenditure

'Rent' to Principal	£32,000	
Professional fees	£1,500	
Insurance	£500	
Clothing/laundry	£500	
Total		£34,500
Profit (without receptionist/telephone answering)		**£29,500**

Sole Practitioner in own premises (rented)
Revenue

Working 4 days a week	£64,000

Expenditure

Rent for premises	£5,100	
Business rates	£2,000	
Printing promotional materials	£2,000	
Professional fees/ training	£1,500	
Advertising	£1,000	
Malpractice Insurance	£500	
Other Insurance	£500	
Equipment (bench etc)	£1,000	
Utilities	£1,000	
Sundries	£1,000	
Clothing/laundry	£500	
Total		£16,100
Profit (without receptionist/telephone answering)		**£47,900**

Receptionist (+ cover)	Cost	£19,000	Profit (47,900 – 19,000)	£28,900
Tel. Answering Service	Cost	£12,000	Profit (47,900 – 12,000)	£35,900

Sole Practitioner in own premises (owned) with receptionist
Revenue

Working 4 days a week   £64,000

Expenditure

Receptionist (+ cover)	£19,000
Business rates	£2,000
Printing promotional materials	£2,000
Professional fees/ training	£1,500
Advertising	£1,000
Malpractice Insurance	£500
Other Insurance	£500
Equipment (bench etc)	£1,000
Utilities	£1,000
Sundries	£1,000
Clothing/laundry	£500

Total   £30,000

Profit (without premises costs)   **£34,000**

Converted room at home

Cost   £2,100   (£34,000 - £2,100)   **Profit with premises £31,900**

With Extension at home

Higher Cost   £8,500   (£34,000 - £8,500)   **Profit with premises £25,500**

Lower Cost   £1,800   (£34,000 - £1,800)   **Profit with premises £32,200**

Purchasing a property

Higher Cost   £30,400   (£34,000 - £30,400)   **Profit with premises £3,600**

Lower Cost   £19,000   (£34,000 - £19,000)   **Profit with premises £15,000**

Please note that these property-related examples show a range of budgets and your own situation may lie within or outside that range, depending on circumstances. The lower profit (and therefore income) should also be balanced against the increased value of property – especially if a distinct property is purchased. No allowance has been made for changes in property values as this is outside the scope of this Handbook.

Sole Practitioner in own premises (owned) with telephone answering service

Revenue

Working 4 days a week	£64,000

Expenditure

Tel. Answering Service	£12,000	
Business rates	£2,000	
Printing promotional materials	£2,000	
Professional fees/ training	£1,500	
Advertising	£1,000	
Malpractice Insurance	£500	
Other Insurance	£500	
Equipment (bench etc)	£1,000	
Utilities	£1,000	
Sundries	£1,000	
Clothing/laundry	£500	
Total		£23,000
Profit (without premises costs)		**£41,000**

Converted room at home

Cost	£2,100	(£41,000- £2,100)	**Profit with premises £38,900**

With Extension at home

Higher Cost	£8,500	(£41,000 - £8,500)	**Profit with premises £32,500**
Lower Cost	£1,800	(£41,000 - £1,800)	**Profit with premises £39,200**

Purchasing a property

Higher Cost	£30,400	(£41,000 - £30,400)	**Profit with premises £10,600**
Lower Cost	£19,000	(£41,000 - £19,000)	**Profit with premises £22,000**

Please note that these property-related examples show a range of budgets and your own situation may lie within or outside that range, depending on circumstances. The lower profit (and therefore income) should also be balanced against the increased value of property – especially if a distinct property is purchased. No allowance has been made for increases in property values as this is outside the scope of this Handbook.

Principal with associates (renting premises)

Revenue

Working 4 days a week	£64,000

Expenditure

Premises costs (1 treatment space)	£5,100	
Receptionist (+ cover)	£19,000	
Business rates	£2,000	
Printing promotional materials	£2,000	
Professional fees/ training	£1,500	
Advertising	£1,000	
Malpractice Insurance	£500	
Other Insurance	£500	
Equipment (bench etc)	£1,000	
Utilities	£1,000	
Sundries	£1,000	
Clothing/laundry	£500	
Total		£35,100
Profit (1 treatment space)		**£28,900**

Further treatment space for associates then entails additional revenue and expenditure:

1 extra treatment space (27 m²) would entail additional rent of £4,050 and business rates of £1,620 – totalling £5,670

If that extra space were used by an associate 1 day a week:

Rent/Rates	£5,670	'Rent' from Assoc.	£8,000	
Additional Profit			(£8,000 – 5,670)	**£2,330**

If that extra space were used by one or more associates 2 days a week:

Rent/Rates	£5,670	'Rent' from Assoc.	£16,000	
Additional Profit			(£16,000 – 5,670)	**£10,330**

If that extra space were used by one or more associates 3 days a week:

Rent/Rates	£5,670	'Rent' from Assoc.	£24,000	
Additional Profit			(£24,000 – 5,670)	**£18,330**

Principal with associates (own premises)

Revenue

Working 4 days a week	£64,000

Expenditure

Premises costs (highest assumed cost)	£30,400
Receptionist (+ cover)	£19,000
Business rates	£2,000
Printing promotional materials	£2,000
Professional fees/ training	£1,500
Advertising	£1,000
Malpractice Insurance	£500
Other Insurance	£500
Equipment (bench etc)	£1,000
Utilities	£1,000
Sundries	£1,000
Clothing/laundry	£500

Total	£60,400
Profit (highest assumed cost)	**£3,600**

This highest-cost building would include extra treatment space, so having associates would only entail additional revenue (though some marginal costs of equipment, laundry and sundries would increase):

The additional rent from each associate/day would be £8,000, so it is easy to calculate additional profit:

One extra treatment space used 1 day a week	**Total Profit**	**£11,600**
One extra treatment space used 2 days a week	**Total Profit**	**£19,600**
One extra treatment space used 3 days a week	**Total Profit**	**£27,600**
One extra treatment space used 4 days a week	**Total Profit**	**£35,600**
One extra treatment space used 5 days a week	**Total Profit**	**£43,600**
One extra treatment space used 6 days a week	**Total Profit**	**£51,600**

If extra treatment spaces were added, it is clear how total profit would grow (though, of course, larger practices would require greater infrastructure – more receptionists, practice managers etc).

This section illustrates that there are many different ways of creating your vision, all of which will have varying revenue, cost, profit and capital implications. Understanding these and considering the various scenarios alongside your own attitude to risk will ensure the right balance between financial security and entrepreneurial risk. You may wish to consult an accountant or business consultant when making those considerations.

Useful Contacts

Accountants

Fizz Accounting Limited
Jane Park and Greg Lovett
01844 358007
mail@fizzhq.com
www.fizzhq.com

RA Accountants
Riz Akhtar
0208 429 7474
info@raaccountants.com
www.raaccountants.com

Knox and Eames Chartered Accountants
Su Knox
01491 628182
Su@knoxandeames.co.uk
www.knoxandeames.co.uk

Brand Identity, graphic, print and web design

Brand New Dawn
Dawn Lillington
01865 400640
dawn@brandnewdawn.com
www.brandnewdawn.com

Herald Chase Group
Chris Goslar
0118 947 4888
chris.goslar@heraldchase.com
www.heraldchase.com

Copywriters

Wrightcopy Limited
Liz Wright
07769 892084
liz@wrightcopy.co.uk

Moving Finger
Christopher Snowden
0845 519 5537
chris@movingfinger.co.uk
www.movingfinger.co.uk

Credit Card Machine Providers

Streamline
www.streamline.com
0800 01 01 66

Retail Merchant Services
www.retailmerchantservices.co.uk
0845 241 9960

HR policy, procedures and handling

Indigo HR Consulting Ltd
Louise Farrell
0845 003 9456
Louise@indigohr.com
www.indigohr.com

Gap HR Services
Carolyne Wahlen
0844 588 0301
NoRisk@gaphr.co.uk
www.GapHR.co.uk

Marketing Consultants

Tangram Limited
Christine Rayner
0118 952 6992
christine@tangram.ltd.uk
www.tangram.ltd.uk

Online Newsletter Content Creation

Moving Finger
Christopher Snowden
0845 519 5537
chris@movingfinger.co.uk
www.movingfinger.co.uk

Online Customer Surveys/feedback

Survey Monkey
www.surveymonkey.com

Qype
www.qype.co.uk

Online Newsletter Mailing Services

Constant Contact
www.constantcontact.com
*(To receive a discount on signing-up,
email support@painlesspractice.com
and we will refer you)*

Mailchimp
www.mailchimp.com

Practice Management Systems (Software)

Practicepal
Paul McGee
01303 814949
paulmcgee@practicepal.co.uk
www.practicepal.co.uk

Healthy Practice Vision
Rebecca Mansbridge
01787 881475
contactus@healthypractice.co.uk
www.hpvision.co.uk

TM2
Jeanette Parry
0845 833 1816
Jeanette.parry@insidetm2.com
www.insideTM2.com

Printers

Herald Chase Group
Chris Goslar
0118 947 4888
chris.goslar@heraldchase.com
www.heraldchase.com

Promotional Items (pens etc)

M-four Promotions Limited
Judith Tinker
0845 130 7725
info@m-four.co.uk
www.m-four.co.uk

Search Engine Optimisation for Websites

The Adword Adviser
Jayne Reddyhoff
01235 424716
Jayne@AdwordAdviser.com
www.AdwordAdviser.com

Marketing Resolutions
Olga Landowski
+44 (0) 20 7127 5309
+44 (0) 7919 860 199
olga@marketingresolutions.com

www.marketingresolutions.com

Solicitors

Michelle Harte
Blake Lapthorn Solicitors
01865 254265
michelle.harte@bllaw.co.uk
www.bllaw.co.uk

Telephone Answering

Idealreceptionist Ltd
Leo Meyer
020 8788 6486
contact@idealreceptionist.co.uk
www.idealreceptionist.co.uk

Extra Pair of Hands
Paul Forrest
0118 952 6900
paul@eph.co.uk
www.eph.co.uk

Virtual Admin and Bookkeeping

TC Services
Tracey Colacicco
01491 824521
momashouse@hotmail.co.uk

Website design and creation

Clarihon Web Services
Nigel Day
01579 342360
nigel.day@clarihon.co.uk
www.clarihon.co.uk

The Adword Adviser
Jayne Reddyhoff
01235 424716
Jayne@AdwordAdviser.com
www.AdwordAdviser.com

Workplace and Personal Insurance Providers

Western Provident Association (WPA)
Lorna Smith
07807 202822
Lorna.smith@wpa.org.uk
www.wpa.org.uk/lornasmith